UNDERSTANDING TOURISM

By the same author

Britain – Workshop or Service Centre to the World?
The British Hotel and Catering Industry
The Business of Hotels
Dictionary of Travel, Tourism and Hospitality
Europeans on Holiday
Higher Education and Research in Tourism in Western Europe
Historical Development of Tourism (with A.J. Burkart)
Holiday Surveys Examined
The Management of Tourism (with A.J. Burkart eds.)
Managing Tourism (ed.)
A Manual of Hotel Reception (with J.R.S. Beavis)
Paying Guests
Profile of the Hotel and Catering Industry (with D.W. Airey)
Tourism and Productivity
Tourism Council of the South Pacific Corporate Plan
Tourism Employment in Wales
Tourism: Past, Present and Future (with A.J. Burkart)
Trends in Tourism: World Experience and England's Prospects
Trends in World Tourism
Your Manpower (with J. Denton)

UNDERSTANDING TOURISM

S. MEDLIK

BUTTERWORTH
HEINEMANN

0005854169001

Butterworth–Heinemann
Linacre House, Jordan Hill, Oxford OX2 8DP
A division of Reed Educational and Professional Publishing Ltd

ᴙ A member of the Reed Elsevier plc group

OXFORD   BOSTON   JOHANNESBURG
MELBOURNE   NEW DELHI   SINGAPORE

First published 1997

British Library Cataloguing in Publication Data
A catalogue record for this book is available from the British Library

ISBN 0 7506 3654 8

Printed and bound in Great Britain by
Biddles Ltd, Guildford and King's Lynn

Contents

CONTENTS

Preface

This book has been designed first and foremost for students and teachers of tourism. Students need to know what progress they are making, to test and consolidate their knowledge. Teachers need to know how their students are progressing, what learning problems they have, what parts of the syllabus are going down well or proving difficult; they need feedback. Yet, even a brief look through the pages which follow will show that the book is of interest to others, too – those who make their living through tourism or who simply like being tourists – especially if they enjoy quizzes.

Understanding Tourism comprises 1000 questions, or items as they are called, arranged in ten Parts, which examine the body of knowledge about tourism, and which broadly correspond to most syllabus elements studied in colleges and universities; there are also several tests in a lighter vein and others not intended for the classroom. Each of the ten Parts consists of ten tests of ten items each.

The debate about what comprises the common body of knowledge about tourism continues. In this author's view several aspects appear to be neglected in many courses. First, the meaning and nature and the basic concepts of tourism; tourism still sometimes means what course tutors wish it to mean and terms used are open to different and confusing interpretations. Second, there is often room for a more thorough treatment of tourism statistics; without a knowledge of sources and of the basis on which the statistics are compiled, their correct interpretation is impossible. The third element that is often lacking is a systematic study of the historical development of tourism in the nineteenth and twentieth centuries, without which an important perspective for understanding tourism is missing. A separate part is devoted to each of these three elements in the ten-part structure of this volume to emphasize their importance in the curriculum.

Some three-quarters of the 100 tests have an international flavour and are relevant to tourism teaching and learning anywhere. About one-quarter of the tests focus on particular countries, especially the United Kingdom, and it is less than realistic to expect users in other countries to do justice to them; these are labelled accordingly (e.g. UK, US and so on).

Individual tests and items are of varying difficulty and, therefore, suitable for various levels of course. What represents, in this author's view, minimum essential knowledge for understanding tourism, comprises about one-third, well over 300 of the items, and these are starred *. Almost twice as many, more than 600 items, represent knowledge that may be expected after an in-depth study of tourism, and these are marked †. More demanding questions, country-specific ones, and those mainly included to enliven the repertoire, are not graded.

The questions are asked in such a way that for each there is normally only one predetermined answer. Hence, with few exceptions an answer is right or wrong and no judgement is required in marking the tests. Where more than one answer may be possible, the alternatives are given among the answers.

Several approaches suggest themselves for using this book. Students will find it helpful to test their knowledge of a particular aspect once they have studied the topic; they may also find it interesting to take some tests before as well as after studying the topics, to see the 'added value' of their study. Teachers can use the tests in their present form as printed or draw on the book as a bank of items from which to construct their own tests to meet the needs of particular courses and students. Browsing through the pages is likely to prove both interesting and informative, too, for students and teachers, as well as others.

Most items are based on material published in commonly used tourism texts. My *Dictionary of Travel, Tourism and Hospitality* (2nd edition) covers much of the required knowledge. Other main titles for each part are given in a short bibliography at the end of the book.

I have used many of the items included in this volume in my own teaching of tourism, first at Battersea College of Technology and later at the University of Surrey, in England; during visiting appointments in Australia, Canada, USA and the West Indies; in short courses in Africa and the Far East as well as in Europe; to that extent they have been, therefore, tested.

The material included was also reviewed in its draft form by a panel of contributors to whom I am grateful for their comments and suggestions for improvement. Frances Brown was for a number of years editor of the international journal *Tourism Management*; Terry Coppock is Professor Emeritus, University of Edinburgh, where he was also Honorary Director of the Tourism and Recreation Research Unit; Douglas Frechtling is Associate Professor of Tourism Studies at the George Washington University and was founding Executive Director of the US Travel Data Center; Elaine Leek is a freelance editor who has contributed to several of my books over the years; Allison Roberts has extensive experience of training, teaching and curriculum development in tourism at various levels in the UK and overseas; Chandra Sonpal is Economic Research Manager, British Tourist Authority, and external examiner.

S. Medlik
Guildford, 1997

Part One
Anatomy of Tourism

1.1 Defining Tourism and Tourists

† **1** Which of the following authors is known for the earliest published attempt to define tourism?

    A   W. Hunziker and K. Krapf
        in *Allgemeine Fremdenverkehrslehre* ☐

    B   L.J. Lickorish and A.G. Kershaw
        in *The Travel Trade* ☐

    C   A.J. Norval
        in *The Tourist Industry* ☐

    D   F.W. Ogilvie
        in *The Tourist Movement* ☐

* † **2** Insert the missing words (*business, environment, not more, staying*) in the definition of tourism by the World Tourism Organization (1993) below:

> Tourism comprises the activities of persons travelling to and A......................... in places outside their usual B........................ for C......................... than one consecutive year for leisure, D......................... and other purposes.

† **3** A distinction may be drawn between **conceptual** and **technical** definitions of tourism. Which are used in

    A   surveys?   ....

    B   legislation?   ....

† **4** Which of the following is an essential element of any **technical** definition of tourism?

    A   Expenditure ☐

    B   Mode of transport ☐

    C   Purpose of trip ☐

    D   Type of accommodation ☐

* † **5** Insert the missing words (*destination, regions, tourist, tourists*) in the description of tourism as a system by Australian author Neil Leiper (1979) below:

> The elements of the system are A........................, generating B........................, transit routes, C........................ regions and a D........................ industry.

*†   **6**   Which of the following statements is **true**?

     A   Tourism is synonymous with travel.   ☐

     B   All tourism is a leisure activity.   ☐

     C   Tourism includes travel to work.   ☐

     D   Much tourism involves discretionary use of time and money.   ☐

*†   **7**   Which of the following statements is **false**?
In comparison with international tourism, in many countries domestic tourism is:

     A   much larger   ☐

     B   growing faster   ☐

     C   less regulated   ☐

     D   better documented   ☐

†   **8**   Which of the following are to be regarded as tourists according to the recommendations of the World Tourism Organization?

     A   Air crews staying overnight at the destination.   ☐

     B   Consultants remunerated directly by clients at the destination.   ☐

     C   Members of the armed forces travelling between their country of origin and duty station.   ☐

     D   Students travelling between their home and institution at the beginning of each term.   ☐

†   **9**   Which of the following are **not** to be regarded as tourists according to the recommendations of the World Tourism Organization?

     A   Diplomats travelling between their country of origin and duty station.   ☐

     B   Guests attending weddings and funerals.   ☐

     C   Pilgrims.   ☐

     D   Those visiting friends and relatives.   ☐

*†   **10**   Link each term in the first column with one term in the second to show the most meaningful relationships:

     1   Balance of payments   A   Tourism industry

     2   Resorts   B   Tourist destinations

     3   Tourist facilities   C   International tourism

1st column	1	2	3
2nd column			

1.2 Studying Tourism

Which academic discipline contributes an understanding of the following?

* †   **1**   Supply and demand relationships in tourism

....

* †   **2**   Spatial dimensions and relationships in tourism

....

* †   **3**   Motivations in tourism

....

* †   **4**   Government roles and relationships in tourism

....

* †   **5**   Social impacts of visitors on communities

....

What are the following called?

†   **6**   Study of bathing and mineral waters and their healing effects

....

†   **7**   Study of the interrelationships between living organisms and the environment

....

†   **8**   Statistical study of populations

....

* †   **9**   Study of weather

....

* †   **10**   Representation of surface features of an area on a map

....

1.3 Types and Forms of Tourism

† **1** The term 'common interest tourism' describes
  A group travel by people with the same interests
  B group visits between 'twinned' towns only
  C a synonym for visits to friends and relatives
  D visits with a purpose significantly shared by the visitor and the visited

*† **2** The term 'cultural tourism' means trips and visits
  A concerned with soil utilization
  B by the educated and discerning
  C motivated by cultural interests
  D in pursuit of learning and scholarship

*† **3** The term 'domestic tourism' denotes
  A travel by indigenous population of a country
  B journeys with stays in private households
  C travel within one's own country
  D coastal travel between ports of a country

† **4** The term 'ethnic tourism' refers to
  A travel by particular racial groups
  B visiting particular racial groups
  C travel by indigenous people
  D visits for ethnic reunion

*† **5** The term 'health tourism' is concerned with
  A treatment of travel-related diseases
  B quarantines imposed by health authorities
  C visits to health resorts and establishments
  D travel by medical and nursing personnel

† **6** The term 'incentive tourism' denotes
  A travel rewarded by commissions
  B travel that has been paid for by a firm as a reward to employees
  C travel stimulated by inducements
  D travel using vouchers to cover spending *en route*

* † **7** The term 'international tourism' applies to
    A   most travel between countries ☐
    B   all travel for which passports are required ☐
    C   travel between countries with different currencies ☐
    D   travel between countries with different languages ☐

* † **8** The term 'mass tourism' refers to tourism
    A   in which large numbers take part ☐
    B   which is promoted through mass media ☐
    C   exceeding carrying capacity of a destination ☐
    D   consisting of travel to mass meetings ☐

* † **9** The term 'rural tourism'
    A   is synonymous with agricultural tourism ☐
    B   describes travel by residents of rural areas ☐
    C   refers to travel to countryside destinations ☐
    D   means travel between rural destinations ☐

* † **10** The term 'urban tourism' describes
    A   business travel ☐
    B   travel by residents of urban areas ☐
    C   travel to town and city destinations ☐
    D   travel between towns and cities ☐

1.4 Propensities, Determinants, Motivations

† **1** In a country with a population of 55 million, 33 million people took 44 million holiday (vacation) trips in a year. What was

    A   the net holiday (vacation) propensity?   ....

    B   the gross holiday (vacation) propensity?   ....

    C   the holiday (vacation) frequency?   ....

* †   **2** What is the single most important determinant of the holiday (vacation) propensity in a country?

    A   Car ownership   ☐

    B   Second home ownership   ☐

    C   Standard of living   ☐

    D   Urbanization   ☐

* †   **3** Available evidence suggests that holiday (vacation) propensity generally increases with

    A   age   ☐

    B   size of household   ☐

    C   unemployment   ☐

    D   level of education   ☐

†   **4** Which of the following are demand determinants (D) and which are supply determinants (S) in tourism?

    A   Availability of tourism accommodation   ....

    B   Degree of urbanization   ....

    C   Level of air fares   ....

    D   Occupational distribution of the population   ....

* †   **5** An increase in the value of a country's currency against all other currencies is generally likely to

    A   decrease the country's residents' travel abroad   ☐

    B   have no effect on residents' travel abroad   ☐

    C   decrease arrivals from other countries   ☐

    D   have no effect on arrivals   ☐

†   **6** The push–pull theory was originally developed to explain

    A   migration   ☐

    B   motivation to work   ☐

    C   need for social interaction   ☐

    D   why people travel   ☐

† 7 Which of the following is true of Maslow's needs theory?

A It was developed to explain tourist behaviour. ☐

B It applies to leisure but not to work behaviour. ☐

C It states that human needs as motivators form a hierarchy. ☐

D It suggests that one has to satisfy fully the needs at one level before moving on to the next. ☐

† 8 In his personality theory of tourist behaviour, American researcher Stanley Plog distinguishes between types of traveller. What are the extremes called?

A One with a preference for exploration and inquisitiveness, exotic destinations and unstructured vacations is called

....

B One who is not adventurous and wants security, prefers familiar destinations, tourist areas and package tours is called

....

† 9 Which of the following show primarily sunlust motivations (S) and which show primarily wanderlust motivations (W), as defined by American author H. P. Gray (1970)?

A An African on a sightseeing tour of Europe ....

B An American on a safari in Africa ....

C A German on a beach holiday (vacation) on the Italian Riviera ....

D A Scotsman on a skiing holiday (vacation) in the French Alps ....

† 10 The term 'conspicuous consumption', as defined by American economist Thorstein Veblen (1899), refers to purchases

A of consumer goods and services generally ☐

B of consumer durables ☐

C which satisfy a physical need ☐

D which satisfy a psychological need ☐

1.5 Describing People

Note: This test may be attempted with or without reference to the following list: alien, citizen, commuter, day visitor, emigrant, excursionist, exile, expatriate, guest worker, national, nomad, overnight visitor, (same) day visitor, stayover visitor, tourist.

What term describes a person who

* †   **1**   is a member of a state by birth or naturalization?

....

* †   **2**   moves voluntarily away from his/her native country to take up permanent residence in another country?

....

†   **3**   lives voluntarily away from his/her country of citizenship?

....

* †   **4**   is compelled by political or other circumstances to live away from his/her native country?

....

* †   **5**   is a visitor staying at least one night in the place visited?

....

* †   **6**   is a visitor not staying overnight in the place visited?

....

* †   **7**   is not a citizen of the country of his/her residence?

....

†   **8**   moves temporarily to another country for employment?

....

†   **9**   lives a wandering life?

....

* †   **10**   travels regularly between his/her place of residence and work?

....

1.6 Tourism Concepts

Underline which is the wider concept in each of the following pairs:

†	1	A	common interest tourism	B	visits to friends and relatives
* †	2	A	destination	B	resort
†	3	A	discretionary income	B	disposable income
* †	4	A	domestic tourism	B	internal tourism
* †	5	A	domestic tourism	B	national tourism
†	6	A	farm tourism	B	rural tourism
* †	7	A	health tourism	B	spa tourism
* †	8	A	leisure	B	recreation
* †	9	A	tourist	B	visitor
* †	10	A	traveller	B	visitor

1.7 Tourism Synonyms

Give a synonym for each of the following terms:

† **1** citizen

....

* † **2** excursionist

....

* † **3** industrialized countries

....

* † **4** package tour

....

† **5** permanent residence

....

† **6** responsible tourism

....

* † **7** service industries

....

* † **8** Third World countries

....

† **9** tour operator

....

† **10** tourism sector

....

1.8 Tourism Opposites

Give the opposite of each of the following terms:

* † **1** business travel

....

* † **2** domestic tourism

....

* † **3** emigrant

....

* † **4** group travel

....

* † **5** inbound tourism

....

* † **6** inclusive tour

....

* † **7** main holiday (vacation)

....

* † **8** overnight visit

....

* † **9** tourist generating area

....

* † **10** urban tourism

....

1.9 US versus UK Language   US/UK

Give the UK equivalents of the following American terms:

1 auto rental

....

2 automobile

....

3 campground

....

4 lodging industry

....

5 motor home

....

6 price/rate hike

....

7 railroad

....

8 vacation

....

9 vacation home

....

10 vacation trip

....

1.10 The Language North of the Border UK

Give the Scottish term for:

1 a deep narrow valley, usually forming the course of a stream

....

2 a wide valley or low-lying flat land bounded by hills or high ground

....

3 a narrow channel between two islands or an island and the mainland

....

4 a lake or arm of the sea, especially if bounded by steep sides or partly landlocked

....

5 a mountain peak

....

6 a mountain over 3,000 ft (914 m) high

....

7 a promontory or headland in Scotland

....

8 an area of coastal water, e.g. arm of the sea, an estuary

....

9 a bridge

....

10 a one-room cottage or hut used as a farmworkers' or shepherds' shelter, nowadays also for walkers

....

Part Two
Historical Development of Tourism

2.1 Worldwide Development

* †   1   Until the early 19th century, the Grand Tour, staying in spas and visiting coastal resorts were, in an embryonic stage, the first manifestations of tourism as we know it today. What did they have in common? All three were
    A   undertaken for health and medicinal reasons   ☐
    B   popular among all age groups   ☐
    C   confined to a small fraction of the population   ☐
    D   in evidence throughout the world   ☐

* †   2   An early major effect of the Industrial Revolution was
    A   increased leisure time of the population   ☐
    B   increased violence   ☐
    C   increased urbanization   ☐
    D   increased conflict in Europe   ☐

†   3   The introduction of railways had a major effect on
    A   decrease in working hours of manual workers   ☐
    B   increase in long-distance stage coach services   ☐
    C   increase in participation in the Grand Tour   ☐
    D   increase in employment   ☐

†   4   The original reason for building piers at coastal resorts was
    A   to break the tidal waves   ☐
    B   to enable steamers to land   ☐
    C   to extend the promenade   ☐
    D   to accommodate entertainment facilities   ☐

†   5   American Express was founded to
    A   assist Americans visiting Europe   ☐
    B   operate a travel agency business   ☐
    C   supply travellers' cheques   ☐
    D   transport money and valuables   ☐

* †   6   The main significance of Thomas Cook's life work lies in
    A   establishing a retail travel agency business   ☐
    B   guide-book publishing   ☐
    C   introducing the hotel voucher   ☐
    D   originating the inclusive tour   ☐

†   **7**   The Suez Canal was built
  - A   to control the water levels of the Gulf of Suez in relation to the Mediterranean □
  - B   to provide water transport between Port Said and Ismailia □
  - C   to shorten maritime routes between Europe and the Orient □
  - D   for irrigation purposes □

* †   **8**   Railway companies in the 19th century, as well as airlines in the 20th century, built and owned hotels mainly in order to
  - A   diversify their respective businesses □
  - B   invest surplus profits □
  - C   provide accommodation for crews □
  - D   safeguard their passenger traffic □

†   **9**   The main effect of population migrations on international tourism has been
  - A   a boost to tourism statistics □
  - B   increased second home ownership □
  - C   increased transport load factors □
  - D   a stimulus to visiting friends and relatives □

* †   **10**   The main cause of the decline of deep-sea passenger line shipping after World War II was
  - A   losses of vessels during the war □
  - B   diversion of ships to cruising □
  - C   growth in air transport □
  - D   lack of investment □

2.2 British Development I   UK

1 Most travel in Britain before the 19th century was undertaken for
  A health treatment ☐
  B pilgrimages ☐
  C business and vocational reasons ☐

2 Which was the first major inland resort in Britain?
  A Bath ☐
  B Buxton ☐
  C Harrogate ☐

3 In which century did seaside resorts begin in Britain?
  A 17th ☐
  B 18th ☐
  C 19th ☐

4 Which was the first major seaside resort in Britain?
  A Blackpool ☐
  B Bournemouth ☐
  C Brighton ☐

5 In which century did hotels first appear in Britain?
  A 17th ☐
  B 18th ☐
  C 19th ☐

6 Which decade has been described as the period of 'railway mania' in Britain?
  A 1820s ☐
  B 1840s ☐
  C 1860s ☐

7 Bank Holidays were introduced in Britain in order to
  A encourage church attendance on major feast days ☐
  B give the banks more time to clear cheques ☐
  C ensure a minimum holiday entitlement for all ☐

8 What was the main form of inland passenger public transport in Britain in the early years of the 20th century?

   A   Bus ☐

   B   Stage coach ☐

   C   Train ☐

9 Which period has been described as 'the golden era of bus and coach travel' in Britain?

   A   1894–1914 ☐

   B   1918–1938 ☐

   C   1945–1965 ☐

10 When did the first large holiday camp open in Britain?

   A   1936 ☐

   B   1946 ☐

   C   1956 ☐

2.3 British Development II UK

1 Arrange the following in chronological order (1, 2, 3):
   A Beginnings of the motor car ....
   B First stage coach services ....
   C First railway construction ....

2 Arrange the following types of tourism accommodation in the order of their first appearance in Britain (1, 2, 3):
   A Motels ....
   B Hotels ....
   C Inns ....

3 Thomas Cook scored most of his 'firsts' between 1840 and 1880. Arrange the following in chronological order (1, 2, 3):
   A First round-the-world tour ....
   B First hotel coupon issue ....
   C First major excursion to London ....

4 Arrange the following events in chronological order (1, 2, 3):
   A The setting up of the Countryside Commission ....
   B The passing of the first Town and Country Planning Act ....
   C The foundation of the National Trust ....

5 Arrange the following national tourism bodies in the order in which they were established (1, 2, 3):
   A English Tourist Board ....
   B Scottish Travel Association ....
   C Wales Tourist and Holidays Board ....

6 Three major events brought large numbers of visitors to London within a few years in the late 1940s and early 1950s – in what order (1, 2, 3)?
   A Coronation of Queen Elizabeth II ....
   B Festival of Britain ....
   C Olympic Games ....

7 In what order did the following post–World War II hotels open (1, 2, 3)?
   A London Hilton, highest hotel in Britain ....
   B Skyway, first major hotel at London Heathrow ....
   C Westbury, first new large London hotel ....

8　The first three major hotel cooperative marketing groups were formed in Britain in the 1960s – in what order (1, 2, 3)?

　　A　Inter Hotels　　　　　　　　　　　　　　　　..........

　　B　Interchange Hotels　　　　　　　　　　　　..........

　　C　Prestige Hotels　　　　　　　　　　　　　..........

9　In what order did the following transport developments occur (1, 2, 3)?

　　A　Opening of the Channel Tunnel　　　　　　..........

　　B　Advanced Passenger Train entry into service　..........

　　C　Opening of the first motorway (M1)　　　　..........

10　In what order were the following airports opened (1, 2, 3)?

　　A　London City Airport　　　　　　　　　　　..........

　　B　Gatwick Airport　　　　　　　　　　　　　..........

　　C　Stansted Airport as London's 3rd airport　　..........

2.4 American Development

When

1 was the first railway opened in the USA?
   A   1810   ☐
   B   1830   ☐
   C   1850   ☐

2 was American Express founded?
   A   1830   ☐
   B   1850   ☐
   C   1870   ☐

3 was Yellowstone National Park established?
   A   1842   ☐
   B   1872   ☐
   C   1902   ☐

4 did the first scheduled air service begin in the USA?
   A   1905   ☐
   B   1915   ☐
   C   1925   ☐

5 did the first motels appear in North America?
   A   1905   ☐
   B   1915   ☐
   C   1925   ☐

6 was Hoover Dam built?
   A   1920s   ☐
   B   1930s   ☐
   C   1940s   ☐

7 did Hilton Hotels acquire Statler Hotels?
   A   1934   ☐
   B   1954   ☐
   C   1974   ☐

8 did Disneyland, California, first open?
- A 1945 ☐
- B 1955 ☐
- C 1965 ☐

9 did air transport deregulation begin in the USA?
- A 1968 ☐
- B 1978 ☐
- C 1988 ☐

10 did the North American Free Trade Agreement (NAFTA) come into effect?
- A 1974 ☐
- B 1984 ☐
- C 1994 ☐

2.5 Transport Development

* † **1** When was the world's first passenger railway opened?
    A   1830 ☐
    B   1840 ☐
    C   1850 ☐

* † **2** When did a regular steamship service begin on the North Atlantic?
    A   1740 ☐
    B   1840 ☐
    C   1940 ☐

  † **3** When was the Suez Canal opened?
    A   1839 ☐
    B   1869 ☐
    C   1899 ☐

  † **4** When did a daily air service begin between London and Paris?
    A   1919 ☐
    B   1929 ☐
    C   1939 ☐

  † **5** When was the first commercial air service introduced on the North Atlantic?
    A   1929 ☐
    B   1939 ☐
    C   1949 ☐

  † **6** When were economy class air fares introduced on the North Atlantic?
    A   1947 ☐
    B   1957 ☐
    C   1967 ☐

  † **7** When were tourist class air fares introduced on the North Atlantic?
    A   1945 ☐
    B   1952 ☐
    C   1959 ☐

* † **8** When did North Atlantic passenger air traffic first exceed sea traffic?

  A 1947 □

  B 1957 □

  C 1967 □

† **9** When was Laker Airways Skytrain launched on the North Atlantic?

  A 1967 □

  B 1977 □

  C 1987 □

† **10** When did Air France and British Airways begin transatlantic Concorde services?

  A 1966 □

  B 1976 □

  C 1986 □

2.6 World Events since 1945

When did the following events occur?

1 Beginning of the Berlin airlift

....

2 Outbreak of the Korean War

....

3 Hungarian uprising

....

4 Suez crisis

....

5 Six Day War between Egypt and Israel

....

6 Warsaw Pact invasion of Czechoslovakia

....

7 Outbreak of conflict in Northern Ireland

....

8 Falklands War between the UK and Argentina

....

9 Collapse of the Soviet Union

....

10 Gulf War

....

2.7 World Tourism since 1945

In which year

1   was IATA founded (reconstituted)?

....

2   was the first Bermuda Air Agreement made between the USA and the UK?

....

3   was the European Travel Commission founded?

....

4   were the first jet aircraft services introduced on the North Atlantic?

....

5   did the first United Nations Conference on International Travel and Tourism take place?

....

6   was the International Tourist Year?

....

7   was the World Tourism Organization established?

....

8   was the European Year of Tourism?

....

9   did the annual international tourist arrivals exceed 500 million for the first time?

....

10   was the Eurotunnel officially opened?

....

2.8 Who Was Who in Tourism Worldwide

Who

† **1** was the author of *The Innocents Abroad*?

....

2 pioneered the first regular transatlantic steamship service?

....

† **3** was the best-known 19th century tourist guide publisher?

....

† **4** built the first modern sleeping and dining rail cars?

....

† **5** was the original founder of American Express?

....

† **6** introduced skiing to Switzerland?

....

† **7** was described as 'Hotelkeeper to Kings and King of Hotelkeepers'?

....

† **8** said that there were only three rules for success in the hotel business –
location, location, location?

....

† **9** founded the organization which created the world's largest theme
parks?

....

† **10** operated the Skytrain on the North Atlantic?

....

2.9 Who Was Who in British Tourism   UK

Who

1   was known as 'Blind Jack of Knaresborough'?

....

2   had a major influence on the grown of seabathing in the 18th century?

....

3   was the first well-known resort publicity officer?

....

4   was described as the 'Father of the Great Western Railway'?

....

5   organized the first inclusive tour abroad?

....

6   was the leading British 19th century tourist guide publisher?

....

7   introduced the Bank Holiday Act in 1871?

....

8   was the author of *Imperial Palace*?

....

9   established the first large-scale holiday camp in Britain?

....

10   produced a report on *The Reshaping of British Railways*?

....

2.10 British Prime Ministers and Tourism UK

Which post-war British Prime Minister

1   told the British people that most have never had it so good?

....

2   reduced the foreign currency travel allowance for British residents to nil?

....

3   could see no reason why anyone should wish to take holidays abroad?

....

4   described hotels and catering as 'part of the candyfloss economy'?

....

5   likened service industries to 'taking in each other's washing'?

....

6   had a holiday home in the Scilly Isles?

....

7   was a keen sailor?

....

8   introduced Selective Employment Tax?

....

9   gave the go-ahead for Anglo-French supersonic aircraft?

....

10   removed all exchange controls in the UK?

....

Part Three
Geography of Tourism

3.1 Introducing Geography of Tourism

Which two countries share

* † **1** the Iberian Peninsula?

....

* † **2** the Scandinavian Peninsula?

....

What are the main gateways for the following global regions?

† **3** East Africa

....

† **4** South Pacific Islands

....

What are the principal places of pilgrimage for

* † **5** Jews?

....

* † **6** Muslims?

....

How many seasons are there in

† **7** the monsoon region?

....

† **8** the polar region?

....

Who 'gains' a day and who 'loses' a day when crossing the International Date Line?

* † **9** Travellers crossing in the western (Asian) direction

.... a day

* † **10** Travellers crossing in the eastern (American) direction

.... a day

3.2 Country Groupings

What are the collective terms for the following groups of countries?

* †   **1**   Denmark, Norway, Sweden

....

* †   **2**   Denmark, Finland, Iceland, Norway, Sweden

....

†   **3**   Fiji, New Caledonia, Papua New Guinea, Solomon Islands, Vanuatu

....

†   **4**   Countries of Eastern Europe and former Soviet Union (former planned economies)

....

†   **5**   Countries of Western Europe, North America, Australasia, Japan (market economies)

....

†   **6**   Countries in the eastern hemisphere

....

†   **7**   Countries in the western hemisphere

....

* †   **8**   Countries bordering the Pacific

....

* †   **9**   Countries bordering the Persian Gulf

....

* †   **10**   Countries of the New World where Spanish or Portuguese is spoken

....

3.3 World's Coastal Resorts

In which countries are the following coastal resorts?

* †   **1**   Acapulco

....

* †   **2**   Antibes

....

* †   **3**   Dubrovnik

....

* †   **4**   Eilat

....

* †   **5**   Malaga

....

* †   **6**   Mombasa

....

* †   **7**   Montego Bay

....

* †   **8**   Rimini

....

* †   **9**   Santa Barbara

....

* †   **10**   Scheveningen

....

3.4 World's Inland Resorts

In which countries are the following inland resorts?

* † **1** Aspen

....

* † **2** Baden-Baden

....

* † **3** Banff

....

* † **4** Chamonix

....

* † **5** Gstaad

....

* † **6** Karlovy Vary (Carlsbad)

....

* † **7** Lillehammer

....

* † **8** Livigno

....

* † **9** Srinagar

....

* † **10** Villach

....

3.5 World's National Parks

In which countries are the following National Parks?

    1 Chitwan

    ....

* † **2** Kakadu

    ....

    3 Komodo

    ....

* † **4** Mount Cook

    ....

* † **5** Peak District

    ....

    6 Plitvice Lakes

    ....

* † **7** Serengeti

    ....

    8 Tikal

    ....

    9 Wood Buffalo

    ....

* † **10** Yosemite

    ....

3.6 World's Heritage Attractions

In which countries are the following heritage attractions?

* † **1** Acropolis

....

* † **2** Brasilia

....

* † **3** Coliseum

....

* † **4** Cordoba mosque

....

* † **5** Great Wall

....

* † **6** Hadrian's Wall

....

* † **7** Mont-St-Michel

....

* † **8** Petra

....

* † **9** Statue of Liberty

....

* † **10** Taj Mahal

....

3.7 Names and By-names of Countries, Regions and Places

What are

† **1** ABC Islands?

....

† **2** ACP States?

....

* † **3** Baltic States?

....

* † **4** Low Countries?

....

* † **5** Nordic Countries?

....

What place is called

† **6** Apple Isle?

....

* † **7** Big Apple?

....

† **8** Big Orange?

....

* † **9** French Canada?

....

† **10** Spice Island?

....

3.8 British Islands and Tourist Regions UK

Identify the following offshore islands:

1 Scenically a microcosm of northern England with archaeological, historical and natural sites, and its own fiscal system

....

2 Scenically a microcosm of southern England with several family resorts and sailing centres

....

3 Around 200 small islands with mild climate, interesting flora and fauna, and unspoilt maritime scenery

....

4 A group of islands with attractive climate, coastal scenery and beaches, and a French flavour

....

5 Britain's most northern island group, with a rugged coastline and a unique culture and way of life

....

Identify the **official English tourist board** regions from their main features listed below:

6 The Broads, heritage, the coastline

....

7 The Cotswolds, Shakespeare's country, the Marches

....

8 Hadrian's Wall, Kielder Forest and Water, heritage coast

....

9 A major National Park, lakes and mountains, popular for active recreation

....

10 Two coastlines, two National Parks, many tourist centres

....

3.9 Scales and Instruments

What scale is used for measuring the following:

† **1** Atmospheric pressure?

....

* † **2** Magnitude of earthquakes?

....

† **3** Strength of wind?

....

* † **4** Temperature, with 100 divisions between freezing point and boiling point?

....

* † **5** Temperature, with 180 divisions between freezing point and boiling point?

....

What instrument is used for measuring the following:

† **6** Altitude both in aircraft and on the ground?

....

* † **7** Atmospheric pressure?

....

† **8** Humidity or relative humidity?

....

† **9** Strength and direction of wind?

....

* † **10** Walking distance?

....

3.10 Abbreviations of Countries, Regions and Places

What do the following abbreviations stand for?

* †   **1**   BVI

....

* †   **2**   EU

....

* †   **3**   FRG

....

* †   **4**   IOM

....

* †   **5**   LA

....

* †   **6**   ME

....

* †   **7**   NZ

....

* †   **8**   PNG

....

* †   **9**   PRC

....

* †   **10**   WI

....

Part Four
Dimensions of Tourism

4.1 Framework of Tourism Statistics

Note: This test may be attempted with or without reference to the following list of terms: inbound, outbound, reimbursed, remunerated, residents, non-residents, three, twelve, tourists, visitors.

Complete the following statements based on *Recommendations on Tourism Statistics* by the World Tourism Organization:

* †   **1** Domestic tourism involves .... of a country travelling in the country.

* †   **2** Inbound tourism involves .... of a country travelling in the country.

* †   **3** Outbound tourism involves .... of a country travelling in another country.

  †   **4** Internal tourism = domestic tourism + ... tourism.

  †   **5** National tourism = domestic tourism + ... tourism.

  †   **6** International tourism = inbound tourism + ... tourism.

* †   **7** All types of travellers engaged in tourism are described as ....

* †   **8** Visitors are sub-divided into .... and same-day visitors.

  †   **9** The stay in the place visited should not last more than .... months.

  † **10** The main purpose of visit should be other then the exercise of an activity .... from within the place visited.

4.2 Basic Tourism Statistics

Note: Questions 1–5 may be attempted with or without reference to the following list of terms: average expenditure per day/night, average expenditure per visit, average length of stay, overnight visits, same-day visits, total days/nights. total expenditure, total receipts, total tourist visits, total visits.

Complete the following equations:

* † **1** Total tourist visits + Total .... visits = Total visits

* † **2** Total visits x Average length of stay = ...

* † **3** $\dfrac{\text{Total days/nights}}{} = \text{Average length of stay}$

* † **4** $\dfrac{}{\text{Total visits}} = \text{Average expenditure per visit}$

* † **5** $\dfrac{\text{Total expenditure}}{} = \text{Average expenditure per day/night}$

Which of the following are **profile** (socio-economic) characteristics and which are **behaviour** (trip) characteristics of tourists?

† **6** Education

....

† **7** Expenditure

....

† **8** Income

....

† **9** Occupation

....

† **10** Purpose of trip

....

4.3 Definitions, Scope and Sources of Tourism Statistics

* † **1** The definition of 'international tourist' recommended by the World Tourism Organization includes *only* visitors who stay in the country visited
A   for leisure purposes □
B   in hotels and similar accommodation □
C   at least one night □
D   for less than three months □

  † **2** Information about the **actual** duration of visit by foreign visitors to a country is most reliably obtained from
A   accommodation records □
B   transport records □
C   a survey of arriving (incoming) visitors □
D   a survey of departing (returning) visitors □

* † **3** The main criterion to be used in the classification of international visitors by place of origin is
A   country of birth □
B   country of issue of passport □
C   country of nationality □
D   country of residence □

* † **4** For purposes of tourism statistics, 'the means of transport' refers to
A   public transport used by a visitor throughout his/her trip □
B   scheduled transport for which payment is made by the visitor □
C   transport used by a visitor to travel from his/her place of usual residence to places visited □
D   local transport used by a visitor at his/her destination □

  † **5** Which of the following items should be included in 'international tourism expenditure' according to the recommendations of the World Tourism Organization?
A   Bank deposits made during a trip □
B   Fare payments for international transport □
C   Cash gifts to relatives during the trip □
D   Purchases of motor cars □

† **6** Estimates of foreign visitors' expenditure in a country are most reliably obtained from

    A   bank records ☐

    B   immigration border control ☐

    C   sample surveys of visitors ☐

    D   surveys of providers of visitor services ☐

* † **7** Which of the following is generally **true** of outbound tourism statistics of generating countries?

    A   They measure all outward travel movements. ☐

    B   They exclude resident aliens. ☐

    C   They measure numbers of visits, not visitors. ☐

    D   They include emigrants. ☐

* † **8** Which of the following statements is **false**?

    A   The number of visits to a destination is the best indication of the value of tourism to the destination. ☐

    B   Total tourist nights are a better indication of the impact of tourism on a destination than total tourist arrivals. ☐

    C   Average daily expenditure provides an indication of the quality of tourist traffic to most destinations. ☐

    D   Average expenditure per visit is a better indication of the quality of tourist traffic to a destination than average length of stay. ☐

† **9** Which of the following forecasting methods draws on group consensus of expert opinion?

    A   Delphi ☐

    B   Extrapolation ☐

    C   Regression analysis ☐

    D   Structural modelling ☐

† **10** Link each term in the second column with one abbreviation in the first column to show which international organization first provided what:

    1   OECD   A   Definition of 'visitor'

    2   IMF   B   Classification of international payments

    3   WTO   C   Common framework for national holiday (vacation) surveys

1st column	1	2	3
2nd column			

4.4 Patterns of International Tourism

Note: Questions and answers are based on data published by the World
Tourism Organization (WTO) and refer to the mid-1990s.

† **1** In the mid-1990s total international tourist arrivals worldwide were in
the range
A   300–400 million ☐
B   400–500 million ☐
C   500–600 million ☐
D   600–700 million ☐

* † **2** What is the main purpose of travel in international tourism?
A   Business ☐
B   Holiday (vacation) ☐
C   Visiting friends and relatives ☐
D   Other ☐

* † **3** The main international tourist flows are
A   between developed countries ☐
B   between developing countries ☐
C   from developed to developing countries ☐
D   from developing to developed countries ☐

* † **4** Most international tourist movements in the world take place
A   across the North Atlantic ☐
B   between English-speaking countries ☐
C   within the Americas ☐
D   within Europe ☐

* † **5** Which global destination region receives most international arrivals
and receipts?
A   Africa ☐
B   Americas ☐
C   East Asia & Pacific ☐
D   Europe ☐

* †   **6**   Which is the fastest growing global destination region in international tourism?

     A   Africa ☐

     B   Americas ☐

     C   East Asia & Pacific ☐

     D   Europe ☐

†   **7**   Which country receives the highest number of international tourist arrivals?

     A   France ☐

     B   Italy ☐

     C   Spain ☐

     D   USA ☐

†   **8**   Which country earns the largest international tourism receipts?

     A   France ☐

     B   Italy ☐

     C   Spain ☐

     D   USA ☐

†   **9**   Which country generates the highest number of trips abroad?

     A   Germany ☐

     B   Japan ☐

     C   United Kingdom ☐

     D   USA ☐

†   **10**   Which country generates the largest expenditure on travel abroad?

     A   Germany ☐

     B   Japan ☐

     C   United Kingdom ☐

     D   USA ☐

4.5 Tourism-related Surveys in the UK   UK

Which survey provides information about

1 day trips of British residents in Britain?

....

2 volume and value of overnight trips of UK residents?

....

3 employment and self-employment in British tourism-related industries?

....

4 expenditure of private households in Britain?

....

5 long holidays (vacations, 4 nights or more) of British residents abroad?

....

6 numbers, length of stay and spending of overseas visitors to the UK?

....

7 personal travel patterns of British residents in Britain?

....

8 readership of British newspapers and periodicals?

....

9 short holidays (vacations, 1–3 nights) of UK residents in the UK?

....

10 UK residents' travel abroad for all purposes?

....

4.6 UK Tourism in Figures   UK

Note: Questions and answers refer to results of the United Kingdom Tourism
Survey (UKTS), which covers **tourism for all purposes by UK
residents of one or more nights away from home**. The Survey
collects data about both UK and non-UK travel but its main value is in
the information it provides about domestic tourism. Questions and
answers refer to the mid-1990s.

1   In recent years the annual total number of tourism trips by UK
residents in the UK has been in the region of
A   100 million+   ☐
B   200 million+   ☐
C   300 million+   ☐

2   The average length of tourism trips by UK residents in the UK has
been about
A   4 nights   ☐
B   7 nights   ☐
C   10 nights   ☐

3   The total number of short tourism trips (1–3 nights) has been in
comparison with long trips (4 nights or more) each year
A   much larger   ☐
B   much smaller   ☐
C   about the same   ☐

4   Which is the most popular tourism destination region for UK residents
within the UK?
A   Scotland   ☐
B   Wales   ☐
C   West Country   ☐

5   What is the main purpose of tourism trips by UK residents in the UK?
A   Business   ☐
B   Holiday (vacation)   ☐
C   Visiting friends or relatives (VFR)   ☐

6 Which part of the UK other than England generates most trips by UK residents in the UK?

A   Scotland   ☐

B   Wales   ☐

C   Northern Ireland   ☐

7 What is the most frequently used method of transport by UK residents to reach their tourism destination in the UK?

A   Bus/coach   ☐

B   Car   ☐

C   Train   ☐

8 What is the most popular type of accommodation used by UK residents on tourism trips in the UK?

A   Friends'/relatives' home   ☐

B   Self-catering accommodation   ☐

C   Serviced accommodation   ☐

9 What is the largest single element of British residents' spending on tourism trips in the UK?

A   Accommodation   ☐

B   Eating out   ☐

C   Travel   ☐

10 Which type of location attracts most tourism spending by UK residents travelling in the UK?

A   Countryside   ☐

B   Towns   ☐

C   Seaside   ☐

4.7 UK in International Tourism   UK

Note: Questions and answers refers to results of the International Passenger Survey (IPS), the principal source of statistics of incoming and outgoing travel and tourism to and from the UK; the IPS results are supplemented by estimates of travel between the UK and the Republic of Ireland and of earnings and expenditure for the Channel Islands.

1   The total number of visits by overseas residents to the UK in the mid-1990s was
   A   less than 20 million   ☐
   B   20–30 million   ☐
   C   more than 30 million   ☐

2   Which overseas country generates the largest number of visits to the UK?
   A   France   ☐
   B   Germany   ☐
   C   USA   ☐

3   What is the most frequently used form of transport by overseas visitors to arrive in the UK?
   A   Air   ☐
   B   Sea   ☐
   C   Channel Tunnel   ☐

4   What is the main purpose of visit by overseas residents to the UK?
   A   Business   ☐
   B   Holiday (vacation)   ☐
   C   Visiting friends or relatives (VFR)   ☐

5   What proportion of visits to the UK by overseas residents is on inclusive tours?
   A   Less than 10%   ☐
   B   10–20%   ☐
   C   More than 20%   ☐

6 The total number of visits abroad by UK residents in the mid-1990s was

A   less than 35 million ☐

B   35–45 million ☐

C   more than 45 million ☐

7 Which overseas country receives the largest number of visits from UK residents?

A   France ☐

B   Spain ☐

C   USA ☐

8 What is the most frequently used form of transport by UK residents leaving the UK?

A   Air ☐

B   Sea ☐

C   Channel Tunnel ☐

9 What is the main purpose of visits abroad by UK residents?

A   Business ☐

B   Holiday (vacation) ☐

C   Visiting friends or relatives (VFR) ☐

10 What proportion of visits abroad by UK residents is on inclusive tours?

A   Less than 30% ☐

B   Between 30% and 50% ☐

C   More than 50% ☐

4.8 USA in International Tourism   US

Note: Questions and answers are based on data published by Tourism Industries, an office in the International Trade Administration, US Department of Commerce, and refer to the mid-1990s unless stated otherwise.

1   How many international visitors arrived in the United States each year in the mid-1990s?
    A   Less than 40 million   ☐
    B   40–50 million   ☐
    C   More than 50 million   ☐

2   Where do most international arrivals to the United States come from?
    A   Canada   ☐
    B   Mexico   ☐
    C   Overseas   ☐

3   Which overseas country generates most international arrivals to the United States?
    A   Germany   ☐
    B   Japan   ☐
    C   United Kingdom   ☐

4   Which South American country generates most international arrivals to the United States?
    A   Argentina   ☐
    B   Brazil   ☐
    C   Venezuela   ☐

5   Which is the fastest growing market for international travel to the United States?
    A   Canada   ☐
    B   Mexico   ☐
    C   Overseas   ☐

6   What is the US market share of total international arrivals worldwide?
    A   Less than 5%   ☐
    B   5–10%   ☐
    C   More than 10%   ☐

7 Which US state receives most international travel receipts?
A California ☐
B Florida ☐
C New York ☐

8 How does the volume of US outbound travel compare with inbound travel to the United States?
A It is larger ☐
B It is smaller ☐
C It is about the same ☐

9 Which is the main destination for US travel abroad?
A Canada ☐
B Mexico ☐
C Overseas ☐

10 What has been the US travel account balance in the 1990s?
A Positive ☐
B Negative ☐
C Neither (receipts=payments) ☐

4.9 Australia in International Tourism AUS

Note: Questions and answers are based on the *International Visitor Survey*, published annually by the Australian Bureau of Tourism Research.

1 Which is the fastest growing part of Australian tourism?
A Domestic tourism ☐
B Inbound tourism ☐
C Outbound tourism ☐

2 What was the total number of visits to Australia by overseas residents in the mid-1990s?
A Less than 3 million ☐
B 3–4 million ☐
C More than 4 million ☐

3 What was the average length of stay of overseas visitors to Australia in the mid-1990s?
A Less than 20 nights ☐
B 20–30 nights ☐
C More than 30 nights ☐

4 Which global region generates the largest number of visits to Australia?
A Asia ☐
B Europe ☐
C North America ☐

5 Which country generates the largest number of visits to Australia?
A Japan ☐
B New Zealand ☐
C United Kingdom ☐

6 What is the main purpose of visit to Australia by overseas residents?
A Business and professional ☐
B Leisure, recreation and holidays ☐
C Other ☐

7 What is the most frequently used form of transport by visitors arriving in Australia?

A   Air   ☐

B   Sea   ☐

C   Other   ☐

8 What contribution does tourism make to the Australian balance of payments?

A   Less than 10%   ☐

B   10–15%   ☐

C   More than 15%   ☐

9 How many trips abroad were made by Australians each year in the mid-1990s?

A   Less than 2 million   ☐

B   2–3 million   ☐

C   More than 3 million   ☐

10 Between 1985 and 1995 trips abroad by Australians

A   increased significantly   ☐

B   decreased significantly   ☐

C   remained broadly the same   ☐

4.10 The Caribbean in International Tourism
CAR

Note: Questions and answers are based on the annual *Caribbean Tourism Statistical Report*, published by the Caribbean Tourism Organization.

1 Which Caribbean island country has the largest population?
A Cuba ☐
B Dominican Republic ☐
C Haiti ☐

2 Which Caribbean island country has the largest tourism accommodation capacity?
A Cuba ☐
B Dominican Republic ☐
C Jamaica ☐

3 How many tourists (stayover arrivals) came to the Caribbean in the mid-1990s?
A Less than 10 million ☐
B 10–15 million ☐
C More than 15 million ☐

4 Between 1985 and 1995 international tourist arrivals in the Caribbean increased in comparison with total world arrivals
A faster ☐
B slower ☐
C at a similar rate ☐

5 Which of the following groups of Caribbean countries received most tourists (stayover arrivals) in the mid-1990s?
A Dutch West Indies ☐
B French West Indies ☐
C US Territories ☐

6 Which Caribbean island country received most tourists (stayover arrivals) in the mid-1990s?
A Dominican Republic ☐
B Jamaica ☐
C Puerto Rico ☐

7 Which was the most important source of tourists (stayover arrivals) to the Caribbean as a whole in the mid-1990s?
   A   Caribbean   ☐
   B   Europe   ☐
   C   USA   ☐

8 How many cruise passengers arrived in the Caribbean countries in the mid-1990s?
   A   Around 5 million   ☐
   B   Around 10 million   ☐
   C   Around 15 million   ☐

9 Which Caribbean country received most cruise passengers in the mid-1990s?
   A   Bahamas   ☐
   B   Puerto Rico   ☐
   C   US Virgin Islands   ☐

10 Which Caribbean country received most visitor expenditure in the mid-1990s?
   A   Bahamas   ☐
   B   Dominican Republic   ☐
   C   Puerto Rico   ☐

Part Five
Significance of Tourism

5.1 Economic Aspects of Tourism

† **1** What has been the main focus of most studies and research in tourism between 1945 and 1995?
  A   Economic aspects ☐
  B   Social aspects ☐
  C   Environmental aspects ☐

† **2** What correlation is there generally between the stage of economic development and the stage of tourism development of a country?
  A   Positive ☐
  B   Negative ☐
  C   None ☐

† **3** Compared with international trade in goods, how much freedom of movement exists between countries in international tourism worldwide?
  A   It is a relatively free market. ☐
  B   It is a restricted and regulated market. ☐
  C   There is not much difference. ☐

* † **4** Which of the following describes the relationship between demand and supply in most tourism markets?
  A   Stable demand and flexible supply ☐
  B   Volatile demand and flexible supply ☐
  C   Volatile demand and fixed supply ☐

† **5** Which of the following market structures is most common in tourism markets with many small operators?
  A   Perfect competition ☐
  B   Oligopoly ☐
  C   Monopolistic competition ☐

* † **6** Which of the following product characteristics applies to most tourist products?
  A   They are perishable. ☐
  B   They are stored by travel agents. ☐
  C   They are transported to customers. ☐

* † **7** Which of the following is likely to show most price-elastic demand?
   A   Holidays (vacations) ☐
   B   Pilgrimages ☐
   C   Visiting friends and relatives ☐

* † **8** Which of the following is likely to show most income-elastic demand?
   A   Main holidays ☐
   B   Additional (secondary) holidays (vacations) ☐
   C   Convention tourism ☐

* † **9** Which of the following tourist facilities and services are likely to be most labour-intensive?
   A   Car rental ☐
   B   Timeshare holiday (vacation) homes ☐
   C   Travel agencies ☐

 † **10** Which of the following tourist attractions, facilities and services can be expected to experience least seasonal variation in their revenues?
   A   National Parks shops ☐
   B   Resort condominia ☐
   C   Suburban travel agencies ☐

5.2 Economic Impacts of Tourism

Note: Question 2 may be attempted with or without reference to the following list: direct, indirect, induced, primary, secondary, leakages, savings.

† **1** A basic change observed in developed economies has been a shift of economic activity from agriculture and manufacturing to services, including tourism. This means that in such an economy invariably
    A   manufacturing output has been declining   ☐
    B   more people are employed in the tertiary sector   ☐
    C   more foods are imported   ☐
    D   more raw materials are imported   ☐

† **2** Complete the following statements about tourism expenditure impacts:
    A   Tourism expenditure – .... = Direct impact.
    B   Direct + indirect + ... effects = Total impact.
    C   .... effects + induced effects = Secondary effects.
    D   Total impact – .... effects = Direct impact.

* † **3** Which of the following are normally direct (D) and which are indirect (I) recipients of tourism expenditure?
    A   Building firms   ....
    B   Laundries   ....
    C   Railways   ....
    D   Travel agents   ....

* † **4** Rank the following (1, 2, 3, 4) located in a resort area according to the likely dependence on tourism for their business:
    A   Banks   ....
    B   Public utilities   ....
    C   Souvenir shops   ....
    D   Taxis   ....

† **5** Which of the following ratios is the main single indication of the relative importance of tourism in an economy?
    A   Foreign exchange earnings to total exports   ☐
    B   Foreign exchange earnings to exports of services   ☐
    C   Tourism spending to GDP or GNP   ☐
    D   Tourism spending to total consumer spending   ☐

* † **6** Which of the following are Debits (Dr) and which are Credits (Cr) in a country's balance of payments?

    A   Spending by foreign tourists in the country   ....

    B   Fares paid by residents to foreign airlines   ....

    C   Remittances from nationals working abroad   ....

    D   Tourism capital investment in another country   ....

* † **7** Which of the following factors is conducive to high *net* foreign currency earnings from tourism?

    A   High expatriate labour ☐

    B   High foreign investment ☐

    C   High indigenous ownership of tourism industry ☐

    D   High propensity to import ☐

 † **8** Which of the following statements about tourism income multipliers is true?

    A   As long as demand exists for locally produced goods and services, each successive round of spending generates new income. ☐

    B   Simple 'ad hoc' models yield more accurate results than those calculated with input–output analysis. ☐

    C   Regions of a country tend to experience higher multiplier values than countries. ☐

    D   The main value of tourism multipliers is for long-term rather than short-term planning. ☐

 † **9** Which of the following is conducive to low income multiplier values in tourism?

    A   Low diversification of the economy ☐

    B   Low level of imports ☐

    C   Low propensity to save ☐

    D   Low taxation ☐

* † **10** If the employment multiplier of a destination with direct tourism employment of 1,000 people is 1.25, what is the total tourism-related employment?   ....

5.3 Social Aspects and Impacts of Tourism

1 Which of the following groups of local residents has been found in research studies to be most favourably disposed to tourism development?

A   Academics ☐
B   Businessmen ☐
C   Local government officers ☐
D   Police ☐

† 2 The process and the results of interaction between different cultures is described in sociological terms as

A   acclimatization ☐
B   acculturation ☐
C   familiarization ☐
D   naturalization ☐

† 3 The belief that the attitudes and behaviour of one's own ethnic group are superior to those of others, is known in sociological terms as

A   anthropomorphism ☐
B   cultural relativism ☐
C   ethnicism ☐
D   ethnocentricism ☐

† 4 The tendency for an individual or a group to imitate the behaviour of another and to assimilate it as one's own is known in sociological terms as

A   accommodation ☐
B   assimilation ☐
C   demonstration effect ☐
D   replication ☐

† 5 The contempt, dislike or fear of strangers or foreigners or of strange or foreign places is called

A   agoraphobia ☐
B   alienation ☐
C   claustrophobia ☐
D   xenophobia ☐

6 Arrange in chronological order (1, 2, 3, 4) the following stages proposed by American sociologist G. V. Doxey (1976) as a framework for assessing the social impacts of tourism in a destination:

A antagonism ....

B apathy ....

C euphoria ....

D irritation ....

† **7** The term 'social tourism' describes

A tourism to socialist countries ☐

B travel for educational purposes ☐

C tourism which fosters group activities ☐

D assisted holidays (vacations) for disadvantaged groups in society ☐

8 Which of the following has been found endemic to tourism in research studies?

A Alcoholism ☐

B Gambling ☐

C Prostitution ☐

D None of the above ☐

9 Which of the following statements is true?

A Tourism is devoid of cultural enrichment. ☐

B Tourism can be a lever for social change. ☐

C Tourism is the only form of exposure of societies to different cultures. ☐

D Unlike the hosts, tourists are not influenced in their own attitudes and habits by tourism. ☐

10 Is there any evidence for the following statements?

A Tourism is the opium of mankind.
(L. Turner and J. Ash, 1975) YES/NO

B Tourism is a secular substitute for organized religion.
(D. MacCannell, 1976) YES/NO

C Holidays abroad can damage your health.
(P. Rivers, 1972) YES/NO

D Tourism is a passport to development.
(E. de Kadt, 1979) YES/NO

5.4 Environmental Aspects and Impacts of Tourism

† **1** Link each aspect of the environment in the first column with the part of the world in the second column where it is of particular concern:

1	coral reefs	A	Amazonia
2	destruction of forests	B	Mediterranean
3	water quality	C	Africa
4	wildlife	D	Pacific Ocean

Aspect of the environment	1	2	3	4
Part of world				

* † **2** Link each type of pollution in the first column with the main cause shown in the second column:

1	air pollution	A	aircraft
2	noise pollution	B	motor car
3	land pollution	C	sewage discharge into the sea
4	water pollution	D	dumping of waste

Type of pollution	1	2	3	4
Main cause				

* † **3** Link each problem in the first column with the type of location where it is prominent in the second column:

1	erosion and landslides	A	inland resorts
2	oil from motor boats	B	coastal resorts
3	traffic congestion	C	mountains
4	infrastructure overload	D	inland waters

Problem	1	2	3	4
Type of location				

† **4** Link each environmental issue in the first column with one of the effects in the second column:

1 acid rain
2 global warming
3 fossil fuels depletion
4 ozone layer depletion

A higher fuel prices
B risk of skin cancer
C damage to monuments
D increase in sea levels

Issue	1	2	3	4
Effect				

† **5** Give a synonym for each of the following terms:

A green audit

....

B green tourism

....

C greenhouse effect

....

D inexhaustible resources

....

† **6** Link each explanation in the first column with the term to which it applies in the second column:

1 Maintaining something in its present form
2 Protecting from decay and destruction
3 Restoring something to good condition
4 Returning something to previous condition

A Renovation
B Restoration
C Preservation
D Conservation

Explanation	1	2	3	4
Term				

† **7** What are the following types and forms of tourism called?

A Forms of tourism which seek to avoid adverse and enhance positive impacts

....

B Type and scale of tourism considered suitable in view of area conditions

....

C Ecologically sustainable trips and visits which promote conservation

....

D Holidays (vacations) in the countryside working to improve the environment

....

† **8** Assuming typical passenger numbers and load factors, which of the following means of transport uses least fuel per passenger mile?
A Coach ☐
B Jumbo jet ☐
C Medium car ☐
D Train ☐

* † **9** Which of the following recreational activities is least detrimental to the environment?
A Motorcycling ☐
B Snowmobiling ☐
C Water skiing ☐
D Hang gliding ☐

† **10** What are the following awards called?
A European award to destinations with most innovative and effective tourism environmental policies

....

B European award for beaches meeting strict water quality standards

....

5.5 Measures of Tourism Distribution and Impacts

What are the following measures called?

1 Ratio of visitors to residents in an area

....

2 Ratio of tourist beds to resident population of an area

....

3 Ratio of incoming to outgoing tourist flows in an area

....

4 Ratio of nights spent in an area from particular areas of origin

....

5 Ratio of nights spent at a destination to total nights on a trip

....

6 Measure of internal accessibility of a region based on established routes

....

7 Measure of relative compactness and internal accessibility of a region

....

8 Measure of the travel patterns of an origin in relation to destinations

....

9 Measure summarizing data on temporal use levels

....

10 Measure of tourism potential of different regions

....

5.6 Developed Countries and Tourism

Note: Questions and Answers 6–9 refer to OECD member countries and are based on data published in the 1995 edition *Tourism Policy and International Tourism in OECD Member Countries*. OECD covers twenty-nine mainly developed countries in Europe, North America, Australasia and Japan.

† **1** Who postulated that societies passed through five stages of economic development from the traditional society to maturity?
  A John Kenneth Galbraith □
  B Walt Whitman Rostow □
  C Adam Smith □

* † **2** Which of the following is the most commonly used indicator of standard of living in cross-country comparisons?
  A Gross national product (GNP) per capita □
  B Holiday (vacation) propensity of population □
  C Number of cars per 1,000 population □

* † **3** Which of the following characteristics applies to most developed countries?
  A Export trade dominated by raw materials □
  B Fast rate of population growth □
  C Large tertiary sector □

* † **4** Which of the following statements about developed countries is **false**?
  A They have high holiday (vacation) propensities. □
  B They are (not) important tourist destinations. □
  C They are major tourism generators. □

† **5** In which of the following countries has tourism contributed to overall economic development so as to raise it from developing to developed country status in the second half of the 20th century?
  A Bahamas □
  B Cyprus □
  C Spain □

6 What is the approximate ratio of international tourism receipts to the gross domestic product (GDP) in developed countries as a whole?

A   Around 1%   ☐

B   Around 3%   ☐

C   Around 5%   ☐

7 What is the approximate ratio of international tourism expenditure to the private final consumption (PFC) in developed countries as a whole?

A   Around 1%   ☐

B   Around 2%   ☐

C   Around 3%   ☐

8 What is the approximate share of international tourism receipts in exports of goods and services in developed countries as a whole?

A   Around 5%   ☐

B   Around 10%   ☐

C   Around 15%   ☐

9 What is the approximate share of international tourism expenditure in imports of goods and services in developed countries as a whole?

A   Around 5%   ☐

B   Around 10%   ☐

C   Around 15%   ☐

10 What proportion of world trade in goods and services is approximately accounted for by international tourism?

A   Around 7%   ☐

B   Around 10%   ☐

C   Around 15%   ☐

5.7 Developing Countries and Tourism

1 Which of the following Commissions has been particularly concerned with developing countries?
A   Brandt Commission   ☐
B   Brundtland Commission   ☐
C   Outdoor Recreation Resources Review Commission   ☐

* † **2** Which of the following characteristics applies to most developing countries?
A   They are short of land.   ☐
B   They are short of labour.   ☐
C   They are short of capital.   ☐

* † **3** Which of the following statements is **false**?
A   Most developing countries are in Africa, Asia or Latin America.   ☐
B   Many developing countries are island economies.   ☐
C   Most developing countries generate more tourism than they receive.   ☐

† **4** Which of the following is **not** considered to be a developing country?
A   Brazil   ☐
B   Israel   ☐
C   Panama   ☐

* † **5** The main reason why tourism is an attractive development option for many developing countries is because it
A   is a 'clean' industry   ☐
B   earns foreign currency   ☐
C   smooths out seasonal fluctuations in exports   ☐

6 What has been the rate of growth of international tourist arrivals in developing countries as a whole compared with developed countries as a whole in the 1990s?
A   Slower   ☐
B   Faster   ☐
C   About the same   ☐

7 What approximate share of total international tourism (arrivals and receipts) has accrued to developing countries in the 1990s?

A   One-fifth ☐

B   One-quarter ☐

C   One-third ☐

† **8** How do tourism multiplier values in developing countries normally compare with those in developed countries?

A   They are higher. ☐

B   They are lower. ☐

C   They are about the same. ☐

9 Which of the following developing countries receives most international tourist arrivals?

A   Mexico ☐

B   Singapore ☐

C   Thailand ☐

10 Which of the following developing countries earns most from international tourism?

A   Mexico ☐

B   Singapore ☐

C   Thailand ☐

5.8 Tourism and the UK Economy   UK

1 What is the approximate ratio of total tourism spending (see note 1) to the UK gross domestic product (GDP)?
  A   Around 2%   ☐
  B   Around 4%   ☐
  C   Around 8%   ☐

2 What is the approximate ratio of foreign exchange earnings from tourism (see note 2) to total UK exports?
  A   Around 3%   ☐
  B   Around 5%   ☐
  C   Around 10%   ☐

3 What is the approximate ratio of foreign exchange earnings from tourism (see note 2) to total UK exports of services?
  A   Around 20%   ☐
  B   Around 30%   ☐
  C   Around 40%   ☐

4 What is the approximate ratio of total tourism spending (see note 1) to total UK consumer spending?
  A   Around 3%   ☐
  B   Around 6%   ☐
  C   Around 10%   ☐

5 Which of the following industries generates highest export earnings?
  A   Petroleum products   ☐
  B   Textiles   ☐
  C   Tourism (see note 2)   ☐

6 Which of the following economic activities receives most of overseas visitors' spending (see note 3) in the UK?
  A   Hotels and other accommodation   ☐
  B   Retailing   ☐
  C   Transport   ☐

7 Which of the following economic activities receives most of domestic tourism spending (see note 4) in the UK?

A   Hotels and other accommodation   ☐

B   Catering   ☐

C   Transport   ☐

8 Which of the following economic activities receives most of UK residents' spending on day trips?

A   Catering   ☐

B   Retailing   ☐

C   Transport   ☐

9 How many people are estimated to be directly and indirectly employed in the UK due to tourism?

A   Around 0.5 million   ☐

B   Around 1 million   ☐

C   Around 1.5 million   ☐

10 Every direct job in UK tourism is estimated to give rise to how much employment elsewhere in the economy?

A   Another half-a-job   ☐

B   Another job   ☐

C   Two other jobs   ☐

Notes: [1] Including visitors to the UK and their fare payments to UK carriers plus domestic tourism, excluding day trips.

[2] Including fare payments to UK carriers.

[3] Excluding fare payments to UK carriers.

[4] Excluding day trips.

5.9 Tourism and the US Economy US

Note: Questions and Answers are based on *Economic Review of Travel in America* published by the Travel Industry Association of America. Travel and tourism spending denotes the sum of domestic and foreign visitor expenditures in the USA. In Question 2 'foreign exchange earnings' include international travel and transport receipts.

1 What is the approximate ratio of total travel and tourism spending to the US Gross National Product (GNP)?
A   Around 3%   ☐
B   Around 6%   ☐
C   Around 10%   ☐

2 What is the approximate ratio of foreign exchange earnings from travel and tourism to total US exports?
A   Around 3%   ☐
B   Around 5%   ☐
C   Around 10%   ☐

3 Which of the following US travel-related industries has the highest sales?
A   Air transport   ☐
B   Food service   ☐
C   Lodging   ☐

4 Rank the following US industries according to their receipts (1, 2, 3):
A   Automotive dealers   ....
B   Food stores   ....
C   Travel and tourism   ....

5 How large is the sales multiplier of travel and tourism spending in the USA?
A   Less than 2   ☐
B   Between 2 and 3   ☐
C   More than 3   ☐

6 Approximately how many jobs are supported directly by travel and tourism spending in the USA?

A   Less than 6 million ☐

B   Between 6 and 8 million ☐

C   More than 8 million ☐

7 What approximate proportion of total US non-agricultural payroll employment is directly due to travel and tourism?

A   Around 5% ☐

B   Around 10% ☐

C   Around 15% ☐

8 How much do wages and salaries generated directly by travel and tourism spending in the USA increase as a result of the multiplier process?

A   Less than 2 times ☐

B   2–3 times ☐

C   More than 3 times ☐

9 What approximate proportion of the combined tax revenue of US federal, state and local governments is contributed as a result of travel and tourism spending?

A   2–3% ☐

B   3–4% ☐

C   4–5% ☐

10 Which of the following US Census regions earns most from combined US and foreign visitor spending?

A   New England ☐

B   Pacific ☐

C   South Atlantic ☐

5.10 International Organizations

Below are listed abbreviations of names of international organizations concerned with economic, social and environmental aspects of tourism. What do they stand for?

†   **1**   ASEAN

....

*†   **2**   ILO

....

*†   **3**   OECD

....

†   **4**   TEN

....

†   **5**   UNCTAD

....

*†   **6**   UNDP

....

†   **7**   UNEP

....

*†   **8**   UNESCO

....

*†   **9**   WTO

....

†   **10**   WTTC

....

Part Six
The Tourism Industry

6.1 Tourism as an Industry

Note: Question 5 may be attempted with or without reference to the following list: activities, industries, products, services, domestic, foreign.

* †   **1**   Strictly speaking, what makes up an industry?
    A   Establishments ☐
    B   Firms ☐
    C   Occupations ☐

†   **2**   What is the principal purpose of a Standard Industrial Classification?
    A   To provide a basis for business taxation ☐
    B   To serve as a framework for industry associations ☐
    C   To promote uniformity and comparability of official statistics ☐

* †   **3**   Which of the following statements is **true** of the tourism industry?
    A   It is synonymous with leisure industry. ☐
    B   It is synonymous with hospitality industry. ☐
    C   It is synonymous with tourism supply. ☐

* †   **4**   Which of the following statements about tourism industries is **false**?
    A   The tourism industry may be defined by reference to the market. ☐
    B   Most industries serving tourists are service industries. ☐
    C   Tourism-related industries serve only tourists. ☐

* †   **5**   Insert the missing words in the following definition of the tourism industry by the United Nations Conference on Trade and Development (1971):

    … the tourist sector or the tourism industry … can be broadly conceived as representing the sum of those industrial and commercial
    A .... producing goods and
    B .... wholly or mainly consumed by
    C .... visitors or domestic tourists.

* †   **6**   Which of the following activities forms part of the tourism industry?
    A   Hotel construction ☐
    B   Conference centre ownership and management ☐
    C   Food manufacturing ☐

* † **7** Which of the following characteristics is common to all or most of the tourism industry?

    A   High labour productivity ☐

    B   Low seasonality ☐

    C   Product perishability ☐

* † **8** Which of the following activities usually accounts for the largest proportion of tourism industry employment?

    A   Hotels and catering ☐

    B   Passenger transportation ☐

    C   Tour operations and travel agencies ☐

† **9** Diversification of firms takes place

    A   mainly from tourism into other industries ☐

    B   mainly from other industries into the tourism industry ☐

    C   equally in both directions ☐

† **10** What forms of integration are illustrated by the following?

    A   Merger of two hotel companies

    ....

    B   Acquisition of a wine-shipping firm by a restaurant company

    ....

    C   Acquisition of a travel agency chain by a tour operator

    ....

6.2 Visitor Attractions Worldwide

Note: Question 1 may be attempted with or without reference to the following list: choice, environment, industry, motivation, preference, purchases.

† 1 Insert the missing words in the following definition of (managed) visitor attractions by British author V.T.C. Middleton (1994):
... elements within the A .... that largely determine consumers' B .... and influence prospective buyers'   C ....

† 2 Which of the following describes best the visitor attraction product?
A   The resources offered to the visitor ☐
B   What the visitor buys ☐
C   The visitor experience ☐

† 3 Which of the following factors is most important in determining the size of the market for a visitor attraction?
A   Availability of refreshments and shopping ☐
B   Distance from concentrations of population ☐
C   Variety of activities on offer ☐

*† 4 Which of the following are motivators (M) and which are determinants (D) of visits to attractions?
A   Atmosphere   ....
B   Enjoyment   ....
C   Leisure time   ....

† 5 What are the generic terms for the following groups of man-made visitor attractions?
A   Castles, palaces, cathedrals, churches

....

B   Protected ancient sites, such as fortifications and burial mounds

....

C   Sites and structures identified with mining, industrial processes and past transportation

....

* † **6** Which of the following represents the main source of revenue in most private sector visitor attractions?

A Admission charges ☐

B Meals and refreshments ☐

C Retailing ☐

* † **7** Which of the following is commonly the largest element of operating costs of large new private sector visitor attractions?

A Maintenance ☐

B Payroll ☐

C Promotion ☐

† **8** Complete the following equations, the first a common measure of performance in private sector, the second in public and voluntary sector visitor attractions:

A $$\frac{\text{Total visitor expenditure}}{} = \text{Visitor spending per head}$$

B $$\frac{}{\text{Operating expenditure}} = \text{Recovery rate}$$

† **9** Which of the following places are best known for their site attractions and which for their event attractions?

A Luxor, Egypt ....

B Oberammergau, Germany ....

C Orlando, USA ....

† **10** Which of the following US visitor attractions have regional (R), national (N) or international (I) catchment areas?

A Colonial Williamsburg, Virginia ....

B Disneyworld, Florida ....

C Mt Charleston, Nevada ....

6.3 Visitor Attractions in Britain   UK

Which of the following organizations operates visitor attractions in the public sector (P) and which in the voluntary sector (V)?

1 English Heritage   ....

2 The National Trust   ....

Which of the following visitor attractions has a regional (R) and which has a national (N) catchment area?

3 Blackpool Pleasure Beach   ....

4 Alton Towers, Staffordshire   ....

What method of on-site transport is used at the following visitor attractions?

5 Jorvik Viking Museum, York   ....

6 Wigan Pier, Greater Manchester   ....

Which is the largest and which is the smallest National Park in England?

7 The largest   ....

8 The smallest   ....

What UNESCO World Heritage Site is in

9 Scotland?   ....

10 Wales?   ....

6.4 Transport Modes

Which transport mode offers most prominently the following advantages to tourists over other modes?

* † **1** Sightseeing for groups ....

* † **2** Transporting luggage from door to door ....

In which country is a motorway known as an

* † **3** autobahn? ....

* † **4** autostrada? ....

In which country are to be found the following high-speed trains?

† **5** Bullet Train ....

† **6** Train à Grande Vitesse (TGV) ....

What are the following vessels called?

† **7** A twin-hull boat or ship designed to cut through the waves

....

† **8** A vessel moving above the water surface on retractable submerged fins or foils ....

What form of transport do most foreign tourists use to arrive in

† **9** Canada? ....

* † **10** United Kingdom? ....

6.5 Air Transport

* †   1   Which of the following characteristics applies to air transport?
   A   High labour intensiveness   ☐
   B   Low capital intensiveness   ☐
   C   High fixed costs   ☐

†   2   Which of the following data are used to calculate the revenue load factor?
   A   Gross registered tonnage and passenger capacity   ☐
   B   Load tonne-kilometres and capacity tonne-kilometres   ☐
   C   Passenger kilometres and seat kilometres   ☐

* †   3   Which of the following is described as a transit passenger?
   A   One scheduled to travel on the same vehicle to its final destination   ☐
   B   One who changes vehicle to continue a journey by a connecting service   ☐
   C   One who breaks a journey at an intermediate point   ☐

* †   4   Which of the following statements is true worldwide?
   A   More people fly on international routes than on domestic routes   ☐
   B   Charter flights have higher load factors than scheduled flights   ☐
   C   More charter flights are domestic than international   ☐

* †   5   Which of the following codes used by airlines and others in reservations, time-tables and ticketing consists of three letters?
   A   Codes denoting airlines   ☐
   B   Codes denoting cities/airports   ☐
   C   Codes denoting countries/states   ☐

†   6   What is the equivalent in air transport of the Athens Convention (1974) which limits the liability of shipping companies?
   A   Berne Convention   ☐
   B   Chicago Convention   ☐
   C   Warsaw Convention   ☐

† **7** Which of the following so-called freedoms of the air covers most international point-to-point traffic?

A Cabotage rights ☐

B Technical rights ☐

C Traffic rights ☐

† **8** Which of the following is a cabotage route?

A Los Angeles – Honolulu ☐

B Prague – Bratislava ☐

C Sydney – Wellington ☐

* † **9** The main cause of the decline in transatlantic sea transport after World War II was

A decline in bulk freight ☐

B decrease in European migration to North America ☐

C growth in air transport ☐

† **10** British Airways was formed by the merger of

A British European Airways and British Caledonian ☐

B British European Airways and Imperial Airways ☐

C British European Airways and British Overseas Airways Corporation ☐

6.6 Transport Synonyms and Opposites

Give a synonym for each of the following transport terms:

† **1** back load

....

* † **2** carry-on-baggage

....

* † **3** layover

....

† **4** Plimsoll line

....

* † **5** stern

....

Give an opposite of each of the following transport terms:

* † **6** aft

....

* † **7** charter airline

....

* † **8** starboard

....

* † **9** surface transport

....

† **10** transfer passenger

....

6.7 Hotels and Other Tourism Accommodation

† **1** Which of the following characteristics applies to hotels?
    A   Low capital to revenue ratio   ☐
    B   Low ratio of fixed to variable costs   ☐
    C   High investment intensity   ☐

† **2** What terms describe the following relationships in hotels?
    A   Bed capacity sold and available bed capacity

    ....

    B   Room capacity sold and available room capacity

    ....

    C   Room sales and the number of rooms sold

    ....

* † **3** What is normally the largest element of capital investment in most hotels in developing countries?
    A   Land   ☐
    B   Building   ☐
    C   Interior assets   ☐

* † **4** What is normally the largest single element of hotel operating costs in developed countries?
    A   Consumables   ☐
    B   Overheads   ☐
    C   Payroll   ☐

* † **5** Which of the following statements about hotel accommodation is **true**?
    A   Hotel room occupancies are normally higher than bed occupancies.   ☐
    B   Capital cities tend to have lower annual hotel occupancies than coastal resorts.   ☐
    C   Business centres have normally higher occupancies at weekends than midweek.   ☐

* †   6   Which of the following statements about tourism accommodation is **false**?

A   It determines destination capacity for overnight visitors.   ☐

B   It determines most tourists' choice of destinations.   ☐

C   It influences the choice of destinations by tour operators.   ☐

* †   7   Rank the following tourism accommodation in order of labour intensiveness in operation (1, 2, 3):

A   Motels   ☐

B   Camping sites   ☐

C   Hotels   ☐

* †   8   Categorization of hotel accommodation by type and range of facilities and services is called

A   hotel registration   ☐

B   hotel classification   ☐

C   hotel grading   ☐

* †   9   Link each type of tourism accommodation in the first column with one most likely group of users in the second column:

1   farms   A   students
2   hotels   B   families with children
3   youth hostels   C   package tours

Accommodation	1	2	3
Users			

†   10   What is the world's largest hotel franchise system?

A   Best Western International   ☐

B   Holiday Inn Worldwide   ☐

C   Hospitality Franchise Systems   ☐

6.8 Accommodation Types and Tariffs

In which country is to be found

† **1** a bach?

....

† **2** a gîte?

....

† **3** a parador?

....

† **4** a pousada?

....

† **5** a ryokan?

....

What is the American term for the hotel tariff which includes

† **6** room only and no meals?

....

† **7** room and Continental breakfast?

....

† **8** room and English breakfast?

....

† **9** room, breakfast and one main meal?

....

† **10** room and three meals per day?

....

6.9 Tour Operations and Travel Agencies

* † **1** Which of the following services is normally provided for travellers by **both** travel agents and tour operators?

A Obtaining travellers' cheques ☐
B Obtaining passports ☐
C Obtaining travel insurance ☐
D Obtaining a visa ☐

* † **2** Which of the following usually generates the highest rate of commission for travel agents?

A Airline tickets ☐
B Hotel reservations ☐
C Travel insurance ☐
D Travellers' cheques ☐

* † **3** Which is commonly the largest element of retail travel agency operating costs?

A Administration ☐
B Advertising ☐
C Payroll ☐
D Premises ☐

* † **4** Which of the following statements applies to most inclusive tours?

A The longer the distance, the greater the proportion of hotel cost. ☐
B The shorter the distance, the greater the proportion of transport cost. ☐
C The longer the distance, the higher the tour operator's profit. ☐
D The shorter the distance, the lower the agent's percentage commission. ☐

* † **5** Which of the following statements is true of airlines?

A The travel agent is the only outlet for their products. ☐
B They accommodate inclusive tours on both scheduled and charter flights. ☐
C They never have their own tour operating companies. ☐
D They charge a commission to travel agents. ☐

6 Which of the following is the most important source of revenue of most retail travel agents in northern Europe?

A   Cruises ☐

B   Buses and coaches ☐

C   Railways ☐

D   Inclusive tours ☐

7 Which of the following is the most important source of revenue of most retail travel agents in North America?

A   Airlines ☐

B   Buses ☐

C   Car rental ☐

D   Railways ☐

8 In which country are domestic rather than foreign holidays (vacations) the main source of inclusive tour sales?

A   Germany ☐

B   Japan ☐

C   United Kingdom ☐

D   United States ☐

9 In which country do retail travel agents often assemble specially tailored packages and their own brand of inclusive tours for clients?

A   Germany ☐

B   Japan ☐

C   United Kingdom ☐

D   United States ☐

10 In which country do tour operators often own both travel agencies dealing exclusively in their own products and direct mail systems?

A   Germany ☐

B   Japan ☐

C   United Kingdom ☐

D   United States ☐

6.10 Travel Trade Abbreviations

What do the following abbreviations stand for?

*† **1** ABC

....

† **2** BSP

....

† **3** DET

....

† **4** DIT

....

† **5** FET

....

† **6** FIT

....

*† **7** GIT

....

*† **8** GSA

....

*† **9** IT

....

*† **10** ITC

....

Part Seven
Marketing in Tourism

7.1 The Marketing Concept

Note: Figures in brackets in Questions 1, 2 and 3 indicate the number of letters in the words to be inserted.

† **1** Insert the missing words in the following definition of the marketing concept by US author Philip Kotler (1991):
>   The marketing concept holds that the key to achieving organizational goals consists in determining the needs and wants of A(6).................... markets and delivering the desired B (13) .... more effectively and efficiently than C (11)..................................... .

† **2** Insert the missing words in the following definition of tourism marketing by the Swiss author Jost Krippendorf (1971):
>   Marketing in tourism is to be understood as the systematic and co-ordinated execution of business policy ... to achieve the optimal A(12)... of the needs of B(12) .... consumer groups, and in doing so to achieve an C(11)... return.

† **3** How are typical suppliers' responses to the following conditions in consumer markets described?
A Demand exceeding supply in a sellers' market:
> (10)............................... orientation

B Supply exceeding demand in a buyers' market:
> (5)............................... orientation

C Supply matching demand in a buyers' market:
> (9)............................... orientation

* † **4** Which of the following statements is true?
A Marketing is about consumer orientation. ☐
B Marketing is synonymous with selling. ☐
C There is no need for marketing in a sellers' market. ☐

* † **5** Which of the following definitions corresponds most closely to the usage of the term 'market' in tourism?
A A place where buyers and sellers come together to do business. ☐
B Actual or potential demand for a product. ☐
C A network of dealings between the sellers and buyers of a product. ☐

†   **6**   Which of the following statements is true of most tourist products?
      A   They are composite products.   ☐
      B   They are mostly bought as packages.   ☐
      C   Packaging increases tourists' choice.   ☐

†   **7**   Which of the following statements applies to most visitor attractions as elements of tourist products?
      A   They are invariably free.   ☐
      B   They are a major determinant of tourists' choice of destinations.☐
      C   Each destination offers *either* site *or* event attractions.   ☐

†   **8**   Which of the following statements applies to most amenities (facilities) as elements of tourist products?
      A   They are invariably provided by the private sector.   ☐
      B   They are bought by tourists individually or as part of a package. ☐
      C   They usually determine tourists' choice of destinations.   ☐

†   **9**   Which of the following statements expresses most meaningfully the concept of accessibility as an element of tourist products for marketing purposes?
      A   It means the physical distance in kilometres or miles to a destination from points of origin.   ☐
      B   It is a function of external transport to a destination.   ☐
      C   It is interpreted in terms of the time taken and/or the cost involved to reach a destination.   ☐

* †   **10**   Marketing in tourism takes place at two levels. This means an involvement by
      A   tour operators and travel agents.   ☐
      B   public and private sectors.   ☐
      C   destination organizations and individual operators.   ☐

7.2 Marketing Tools

* † **1** The elements which make up the total marketing operation of an enterprise are called
- A   the business mix ☐
- B   the marketing mix ☐
- C   the promotional mix ☐
- D   the sales mix ☐

* † **2** Market segmentation means dividing the total market into
- A   groups of equal size ☐
- B   groups of equal value ☐
- C   homogeneous groups ☐
- D   heterogeneous groups ☐

† **3** Which of the following segmentation criteria are used in psycho-graphics?
- A   Life cycle ☐
- B   Life style ☐
- C   Social class ☐
- D   Race and religion ☐

† **4** Which of the following pairs of tourist products is likely to be perceived as the closest substitutes by European residents?
- A   Beach holidays (vacations) in Greece and in Turkey ☐
- B   Caribbean and Mediterranean cruises ☐
- C   Pilgrimages to Jerusalem and to Mecca ☐
- D   Skiing holidays (vacations) in Austria and in Colorado, USA ☐

† **5** An omnibus survey is
- A   a survey using questionnaires administered to passengers on buses ☐
- B   a comprehensive survey which covers exhaustively all aspects of a subject ☐
- C   a regular repeat survey which covers a number of topics for different clients ☐
- D   a survey commissioned by or on behalf of a group of clients on a cost-sharing basis ☐

* † **6** Which of the following approaches to product formulation reflects the marketing concept?

    A   Products are shaped to match competition ☐

    B   Products are shaped to match markets ☐

    C   Markets shape themselves to products ☐

    D   Markets and products are shaped by the external business environment ☐

    7 What aspect of product formulation is particularly highlighted in Center Parc holiday (vacation) villages?

    A   Accommodation ☐

    B   Attractions ☐

    C   Food ☐

    D   Location ☐

    8 Semiotics (semiology) is concerned with

    A   Jewish ideas and influence ☐

    B   conveying signs, concepts and images ☐

    C   scientific measurement ☐

    D   study of meanings ☐

* † **9** Which of the following are principals (P) and which are intermediaries (I) in the distribution of tourist products?

    A   Booking agencies ....

    B   Car rental companies ....

    C   Timeshare resorts ....

    D   Conference organizers ....

* † **10** Which of the following statements is true of retail travel agencies as distribution channels for tourist products?

    A   They are the only retail outlets for tourist products. ☐

    B   They are more important in domestic than in international tourism. ☐

    C   They are remunerated by a fee charged to the customer. ☐

    D   Their geographical distribution tends to reflect market density. ☐

7.3 Tourism Promotion

* † **1** What distinguishes publicity from other means of securing public attention?

    A   It seeks to influence potential customers at the point of sale. ☐

    B   The promoter has no control over the message. ☐

    C   The potential customer is known to the promoter. ☐

* † **2** What distinguishes advertising from other promotion?

    A   The advertiser seeks to influence the potential customer at the point of sale. ☐

    B   The advertiser buys space or time in the media. ☐

    C   The advertiser has no control over the message. ☐

† **3** What distinguishes publicity and advertising from other promotion?

    A   They seek to influence the potential customer at the point of sale. ☐

    B   They are personal forms of communication. ☐

    C   Their function is to attract the potential customer to the point of sale. ☐

† **4** What distinguishes sales promotion from other means of attracting the potential customer?

    A   It always takes place away from the point of sale. ☐

    B   The potential customer is never known to the promoter. ☐

    C   It is below-the-line promotion. ☐

* † **5** What distinguishes merchandising from other promotion?

    A   It is an indirect method of influencing potential customers. ☐

    B   It seeks to influence potential customers at the point of sale. ☐

    C   The promoter has no control over the message. ☐

* † **6** Brochures are of major importance in tour operators' marketing communications with customers because

    A   they are a legal requirement in most countries ☐

    B   they act as a product substitute at the point of sale ☐

    C   they serve both as a promotional tool for the operator and as a souvenir for the customer ☐

* †   **7**   **Net circulation** of a newspaper or periodical refers to
       A   the number of distributed copies   ☐
       B   the number of sold copies   ☐
       C   the number of people who read a copy   ☐

†   **8**   In marketing the term **conversion rate** denotes
       A   the number of replies received in response to an advertisement   ☐
       B   the ratio of customers who buy a product to the number of responses received to an advertisement   ☐
       C   the ratio of the number of people responding to the total number approached in a survey   ☐

†   **9**   By whom is an advertising agency normally remunerated in the conduct of a marketing campaign in respect of above-the-line advertising?
       A   The client   ☐
       B   The media   ☐
       C   The printer   ☐

†   **10**   Which of the following may be described as **institutional promotion**?
       A   Direct mailing by a cruise company to members of a professional organization   ☐
       B   Resort hotel advertising in a monthly periodical   ☐
       C   Tourist board publicity in a generating country   ☐

7.4 Pricing Methods and Approaches

What terms describe the following methods and approaches to pricing?

* †   **1**   Setting prices by reference to such criteria as competitors' prices and customers' attitudes, wants and preferences, and adjusting the costs and levels of service to predetermined prices

....

* †   **2**   Setting prices by adding a mark-up to product cost

....

* †   **3**   Charging different prices to different customers for the same product for reasons not associated with differences in the cost of supply

....

* †   **4**   Setting prices to cover the direct (variable) costs and to make a contribution to fixed costs of a product

....

   †   **5**   Setting temporarily very low prices with the objective of driving competitors or keeping new entrants from a market

....

* †   **6**   Setting prices below the commonly accepted level for the product concerned

....

   †   **7**   Keeping selling price at a stable level, i.e., preventing the price from rising and avoiding price reductions

....

   †   **8**   Setting high initial prices in markets with price-inelastic demand

....

* †   **9**   Setting prices with a view to achieving a predetermined rate of return on invested capital

....

* †   **10**   Setting specific or minimum prices for products by suppliers and requiring the distributors to sell at those prices

....

7.5 Pricing Hotel and Transport Services

What do the following abbreviations of transport fares and hotel tariffs stand for?

† **1** AP

....

† **2** APEX

....

† **3** BP

....

† **4** CP

....

† **5** EP

....

† **6** GITX

....

† **7** IPEX

....

† **8** ITX

....

† **9** MAP

....

† **10** PEX

....

7.6 Marketing Applications

† **1/2** Which of the following Caribbean tourist products can be expected to have (1) the largest market and which (2) the smallest market in Europe?

A Beach holidays (vacations) ....

B Cruising holidays (vacations) ....

C Diving holidays (vacations) ....

D Sailing holidays ....

* † **3/4** Which of the following segments is normally (3) most susceptible and which is (4) least susceptible to tourism promotion?

A Study visits ....

B Visits to friends and relatives ....

C Business visits other than conferences

....

D Holiday (vacation) visits ....

† **5/6** Which of the following are usually perceived as (5) convenience products (CP) and which as (6) shopping products (SP) by Europeans on holiday (vacation)?

A Bank services ....

B Car rental ....

C Hotel accommodation ....

D Take-away food ....

* † **7/8** Which of the following destinations may be expected to have (7) the strongest image and which (8) the weakest image?

A Australian Barrier Reef islands among European residents

....

B Mediterranean countries among United States residents

....

C Wales among Japanese residents ....

D Scotland among Canadian residents

....

* † **9/10** Which of the following media is likely to reach (9) the largest market
and which (10) the smallest market in the United States?
A   A newsletter for school teachers ....
B   A national women's magazine   ....
C   A periodical for birdwatchers   ....
D   A student newspaper   ....

7.7 Promotional Illustrations

What aspect of marketing is illustrated by each of the following?

* † **1** Charging lower prices in theatres to students and the retired

....

† **2** Display of travel posters in railway stations

....

† **3** Dividing an hotel market into banqueting, conferences and exhibitions

....

* † **4** Editorial mention of a resort in a periodical

....

* † **5** Grouping chain hotels with unique names and images

....

† **6** 'Happy hour' periods in bars

....

* † **7** Postal distribution of tour operator's brochure

....

† **8** 'Small ads' paid for on a line-by-line basis

....

† **9** 'Spouse-free' travel offer by an airline

....

* † **10** Tent cards on restaurant tables

....

7.8 Creative Marketing Campaigns and Messages

Name the organization identified with each of the following campaigns and messages:

1   'Have it your own way'

....

2   'I love New York'

....

3   'Only one hotel chain guarantees your room will be right'

....

4   'That'll do nicely'

....

5   'The World Next Door'

....

6   'The world's favourite airline'

....

7   'Yes, we're different'

....

8   'We speak your language'

....

9   'We try harder'

....

10   'You're the boss'

....

7.9 Marketing Synonyms and Opposites

Give a synonym for each of the following terms:

† **1** database marketing

....

* † **2** face-to-face selling

....

† **3** niche marketing

....

* † **4** point-of-sale promotion

....

† **5** telephone marketing

....

What is an opposite of each of the following terms?

* † **6** brand switching

....

* † **7** buyers' market

....

* † **8** field research

....

* † **9** market economy

....

* † **10** tactical marketing

....

7.10 Marketing Abbreviations and Acronyms

What do the following abbreviations and acronyms stand for?

†   **1**   AIDA

....

*†   **2**   CRS

....

†   **3**   CSQ

....

†   **4**   DRM

....

†   **5**   GDS

....

*†   **6**   POS

....

*†   **7**   PR

....

*†   **8**   RPM

....

*†   **9**   SWOT

....

†   **10**   USP

....

Part Eight
Planning and Development in Tourism

8.1 Basic Concepts

† **1** What is considered to be the optimum approach to national tourism planning and development?
  A Formulation of a national development plan with tourism as one of the sectors ☐
  B Formulation of a tourism development plan ☐
  C Formulation of a tourism marketing plan ☐

† **2** What is the most common sequence of tourism development in developing countries?
  A Domestic tourism followed by inbound tourism ☐
  B Inbound tourism followed by domestic tourism ☐
  C Concurrent development of domestic and inbound tourism ☐

† **3** What is the appropriate starting point in assembling information for tourism planning and development?
  A To identify available in-house information ☐
  B To establish the exact purpose for which it is required ☐
  C To design a survey to collect the information ☐

* † **4** The term 'community tourism' refers to
  A tourism within the European Community ☐
  B an approach to tourism in which local residents participate in its planning and development ☐
  C group visits between 'twinned' towns and cities in different countries ☐

* † **5** In tourism context the term 'carrying capacity' refers to
  A capacity of a site or area ☐
  B passenger capacity of a bus or coach ☐
  C ship tonnage ☐

* † **6** Which of the following concurrent activities on inland waters are compatible?
  A Angling and power boating ☐
  B Sailing and water skiing ☐
  C Swimming and scuba diving ☐

† 7 How is a land use development strategy which aims to locate particular activities, facilities and services together in an area described?
A Concentration development strategy ☐
B Cluster development strategy ☐
C Enclave development strategy ☐

*† 8 The term 'sustainable tourism' refers to
A level of tourism arrivals which can be sustained over a period of time ☐
B tourism development which commands the support of the local population ☐
C tourism activities which are in harmony with the environment in the long term ☐

*† 9 Which of the following may be classified as infrastructure and which as tourism superstructure in a resort?

A Water supply

....

B Roads

....

C Casinos

....

† 10 For which of the following is the term 'green tourism' a synonym?
A Agricultural tourism ☐
B Alternative tourism ☐
C Rural tourism ☐

8.2 Resources

† **1** It has been suggested that countries and regions should specialize in economic activities in which they have a comparative advantage. This means that they should specialize in tourism if their resources are

A better suited for tourism than other countries'/regions' resources ☐

B better suited for tourism than for other economic activities ☐

C not suitable for any other economic activity ☐

† **2** Which of the following does **not** apply to renewable natural resources?

A They are inexhaustible. ☐

B They are capable of replenishment. ☐

C They are not vulnerable. ☐

* † **3** When referring to both natural and man-made resources, the terms conservation, preservation and restoration are often used indiscriminately. Which of the following describes the essence of conservation?

A Maintaining something in its present form ☐

B Returning something to its previous condition ☐

C Protecting something from decay and destruction ☐

† **4** A study of new resort developments suggests that some resources receive more attention in planning stages than others. Which of the following tends to be most neglected?

A Energy resources ☐

B Manpower ☐

C Man-made attractions ☐

† **5** Which of the following activities makes least exclusive demand on land in most countries?

A Housing ☐

B Industry ☐

C Tourism ☐

* † **6** Which of the following tourism resources is of equal importance for both holiday (vacation) and for business tourism?

A Attractive scenery ☐

B Developed infrastructure ☐

C Pleasant climate ☐

* † **7** Which of the following uses of coastal resorts can be classified as tourism?

    A   As dormitory towns for close urban areas ☐

    B   As second homes ☐

    C   As places of retirement ☐

* † **8** Which of the following is the dominant influence on climate?

    A   Distribution of land and sea areas ☐

    B   Latitude ☐

    C   Relief ☐

* † **9** Which of the following tourism resources is commonly provided by the public sector in developed countries?

    A   Accommodation ☐

    B   Reservation systems ☐

    C   Tourist information services ☐

† **10** Which of the following is the most common multiple use of land resources?

    A   Agriculture and tourism ☐

    B   Housing and tourism ☐

    C   Industry and tourism ☐

8.3 Techniques, Systems and Processes

What techniques, systems or processes are used for the following purposes?

* †   **1**   To assess the market and financial prospects for a new project:

....

* †   **2**   To evaluate the anticipated costs and revenues of a project:

....

* †   **3**   To evaluate the benefits and the costs of a project to society:

....

†   **4**   To plan and monitor complex projects and activities:

....

†   **5**   To schedule component tasks in project planning:

....

†   **6**   To assess the impact of a company's activities on the environment:

....

* †   **7**   To assess in advance the likely environmental effects of a development project:

....

* †   **8**   To reduce the use of electricity, fuel and other energy resources for cost or environmental reasons:

....

* †   **9**   To reduce the use of water resources for cost or environmental reasons:

....

* †   **10**   To reduce waste for cost or environmental reasons:

....

8.4 Ownership and Management

† **1** What is a joint business venture?
   A One party selling a product designed, supplied and controlled by and with the support of another party ☐
   B Involvement of two or more parties in ownership, management, and operation of a business with a participation in financial outcome ☐
   C Provision of organizational and operational expertise to manage a business by an operator for an agreed remuneration ☐

† **2** What is the essence of a concession?
   A Control or ownership of rights to land or buildings over a certain period ☐
   B Right to use land or premises on certain conditions ☐
   C Provision of organizational and operational expertise to manage a business by an operator for an agreed remuneration ☐

† **3** What term describes the arrangement under which an operator takes temporary possession of a property for a specified period of time for rent payment?
   A Concession ☐
   B Lease ☐
   C Management contract ☐

† **4** What is a management contract?
   A One party selling a product designed, supplied and controlled by and with the support of another party ☐
   B Involvement of two or more parties in ownership, management, and operation of a business with a participation in financial outcome ☐
   C Provision of organizational and operational expertise to manage a business by an operator for an agreed remuneration ☐

† **5** What term describes the contractual relationship between two parties for the distribution of goods and services, in which one party sells a product designed, supplied and controlled and with the support of the other party?
   A Franchise ☐
   B Joint venture ☐
   C Management contract ☐

* † **6** Which of the following groups is most interested in the balance sheet of a business?

    A   Management ☐

    B   Owners and lenders ☐

    C   Tax authorities ☐

* † **7** A single physical location at which one or more business activities are conducted is described as

    A   an establishment ☐

    B   a firm ☐

    C   a partnership ☐

  † **8** When a company is acquired by its staff who become shareholders, this is known as

    A   employee buy-out ☐

    B   leveraged buy-out ☐

    C   management buy-out ☐

  † **9** What is described as dual nature of investment in hotels, means

    A   investment financed by equity capital and by loans ☐

    B   investment in land and buildings and in interior assets ☐

    C   investment by two different parties ☐

* † **10** What term describes a building in which the interior space of accommodation units is owned individually and the land and buildings in common by the owners of the individual units?

    A   Timeshare ☐

    B   Condominium ☐

    C   Cooperative ☐

8.5 Reshaping Existing Locations

Note: Figures in questions denote the number of letters in each area/city name.

Which resort has been 'regenerated' by, inter alia,

1 adding a conference centre, a marina and other facilities and attractions (in England?) : 8

....

2 changing image and product identity from a winter to a summer resort (in North Atlantic ?) : 7

....

3 launching a series of festivals and other events (in England ?) : 11

....

4 legalizing gambling (in USA ?) : 8, 4

....

5 transformation into a conference and day visit centre (in the Netherlands ?) : 12

....

Which city has enhanced its appeal to visitors by, inter alia,

6 becoming a European City of Culture and an exhibition venue (in Scotland ?) : 7

....

7 focusing on industrial heritage (in England ?) : 8

....

8 staging several mega-events (in Canada ?) : 8

....

9 rehabilitating its waterfront and other civic improvements
(in Spain ?) : 9

....

10 major waterfront development (in north-east USA ?) : 9

....

8.6 Planning and Development Applications

1 Which of the following visitor attractions in North America is 'user-oriented'?

    A   Colonial Williamsburg, Virginia ☐

    B   Faneuil Hall, Boston, Massachusetts ☐

    C   Disneyworld, Florida ☐

    D   Niagara Falls, New York/Ontario ☐

2 Which of the following visitor attractions in Europe is 'resource-based'?

    A   Fish Market, Bergen, Norway ☐

    B   Lake District National Park, Cumbria, England ☐

    C   Starnberg Lake, Bavaria, Germany ☐

    D   Studio Rampa Theatre, Prague, Czech Republic ☐

3 Which of the following resort areas developed largely spontaneously without much planning?

    A   Cancun Resort, Mexico ☐

    B   Nusa Dua Resort, Bali, Indonesia ☐

    C   South Antalya, Turkey ☐

    D   Venice, Italy ☐

4 Which of the following resort areas was planned ab initio?

    A   Costa Brava, Spain ☐

    B   Côte d'Azur ☐

    C   Lanzarotte, Canary Islands ☐

    D   Pomun Lake Resort, Republic of Korea ☐

*† **5** The main reason for the decline of seaside resorts in northern Europe for domestic holidays (vacations) has been

    A   air and sea pollution ☐

    B   lack of investment ☐

    C   growth in holidays (vacations) in the Mediterranean ☐

    D   lack of promotion ☐

† 6 What effect has the growth of the inclusive tour had on the geographical distribution of holidays?
   A   It has brought about a wider dispersal.   ☐
   B   It has concentrated tourists into specific locations.   ☐
   C   It has had no particular effect.   ☐

* † 7 The population drift from the land to towns in developed countries has been
   A   of relatively recent origin   ☐
   B   mainly caused by tourism development   ☐
   C   often arrested or slowed down by tourism development   ☐

* † 8 Which of the following statements is **false**?
   A   Tourism competes with housing in some places.   ☐
   B   Tourism provides new uses for old buildings.   ☐
   C   Tourism destroys industrial heritage.   ☐

† 9 Which of the following conservation designation schemes applies worldwide?
   A   Environmentally Sensitive Areas   ☐
   B   Ramsar Sites   ☐
   C   Special Protection Areas   ☐

10 Which decade was described as the United Nations Development Decade?
   A   1950s   ☐
   B   1960s   ☐
   C   1970s   ☐

8.7 Planning and Development Terms

Give the appropriate term to describe each of the following:

† **1** Sale of land and buildings by a company to an investor and leasing the same property back for an agreed term

....

† **2** A construction contract that leaves the contractor to see to all details and hand over an operational unit

....

* † **3** Designating areas for different forms of activity

....

* † **4** A formal offer in writing to execute work or supply goods or services at an agreed price

....

* † **5** Industries supplying essential basic public services

....

* † **6** A linear building development along a road, coastline or valley

....

* † **7** Measures of government assistance to encourage firms to invest

....

† **8** Preparing proposals for, and regulating the use of land in a given area

....

† **9** Areas designated by appropriate authorities because of their archaeological, cultural or environmental significance

....

† **10** The cost of an economic activity to society

....

8.8 Planning and Development Synonyms and Opposites

Give synonyms for the following terms:

† **1** alternative technology

....

* † **2** country planning

....

† **3** critical path analysis

....

† **4** timesharing

....

* † **5** urban planning

....

Give the opposites of the following terms:

† **6** enclave

....

* † **7** infrastructure

....

† **8** private cost

....

* † **9** private sector

....

* † **10** urban planning

....

8.9 Planning and Development in the UK

1 Which is the wider concept – Great Britain or United Kingdom?

....

2 The first legislation to regulate physical development in the UK was

....

3 Regulations made by public bodies such as local authorities or railway companies are called

....

4 Local authorities which combine the functions of county, borough and district councils are called

....

5 Plans which combine broad policies and detailed guidelines for some local government areas are called

....

6 Areas of countryside surrounding large built-up areas in which building development is strictly controlled are called

....

7 Areas designated by central government in which businesses benefit from, inter alia, simplified planning procedures, are called

....

8 Statutory bodies set up by central government in order to reverse large-scale urban decline are called

....

9 Initiatives of the English Tourist Board in the 1980s to develop tourism in 'areas of potential and need', were called

....

10 The first major post World War II purpose-built recreation and tourism
centre in Britain was opened at

    ....

8.10 Conservation Areas and Schemes in the UK   UK

In which parts of the United Kingdom are to be found the following designated conservation areas and conservation schemes?
(✔ in the appropriate column)

		England	Scotland	Wales	N. Ireland
1	Areas of Outstanding Natural Beauty				
2	Conservation Areas				
3	Heritage Coasts				
4	Listed Buildings				
5	National Scenic Areas				
6	National Nature Reserves				
7	National Parks				
8	Scheduled Ancient Monuments				
9	Sites of Special Scientific Interest				
10	Special Protected Areas				

Part Nine
Organization and Finance in Tourism

9.1 Types of Organizations

What are the designations of the following organizations?

* † **1** Individual membership organization providing roadside and other services to motorists

....

† **2** Voluntary non-profit making association of businesses in a town or district to protect and promote their interests

....

† **3** Society providing for the survey and classification of ships

....

† **4** Voluntary group of independent firms in a particular trade or industry joined together for marketing or other common purposes

....

† **5** Organization with institutional rather than individual membership, such as an international organization of national associations

....

† **6** Association of employees in a particular occupation to promote their common interests

....

* † **7** Association of individuals in a particular occupation,which seeks to provide status for its members, and which controls admission, usually by examination

....

* † **8** National, regional or local organization variously concerned with the development, promotion and coordination of tourism in its area

....

* † **9** Non-profit making association of independent firms in a particular trade or industry to advance their common interests and to provide services to members

   ....

* † **10** Association of employees whose principal functions include the regulation of relations between them and employers

   ....

9.2 Governments and Tourism Organizations

† **1** Which of the following are normally central government concerns?
A Car parking ☐
B Diversification of local economies ☐
C Economic growth ☐
D Employment ☐

† **2** Which of the following are normally local government concerns?
A Balance of payments ☐
B Employment ☐
C Quality of environment ☐
D Regional balance ☐

* † **3** What is the main distinguishing feature of sectoral organizations?
A They are concerned with particular occupations. ☐
B They are concerned with particular industries. ☐
C They are concerned with tourism. ☐
D They are not concerned with tourism. ☐

† **4** Which is the oldest level of tourism organization?
A Local ☐
B Regional ☐
C National ☐
D International ☐

† **5** Which country first established a National Tourism Administration?
A France ☐
B Italy ☐
C New Zealand ☐
D Switzerland ☐

* † **6** Which of the following is the most common function of tourism destination organizations?
A Industry regulation ☐
B Manpower development ☐
C Marketing/promotion ☐
D Planning and development ☐

†   **7**   What is the main single reason for the involvement of tourism
organizations in marketing?

A   Market fragmentation ☐

B   Need to promote destinations ☐

C   Small scale of many operators ☐

D   Spatial separation between destinations and markets ☐

†   **8**   Where have governments and public sector agencies most intervened
directly in the development of the tourist product?

A   In the First World ☐

B   In the Second World ☐

C   In the Third World ☐

D   In the Fourth World ☐

* †   **9**   Which of the following policy objectives of governments and tourism
organizations are least likely to conflict?

A   Maximizing foreign currency earnings and regional dispersal of
tourism. ☐

B   Maximizing visitor numbers and conservation. ☐

C   Maximizing visitor numbers and attraction of high-spending
tourists. ☐

D   Maximizing visitor revenue and resident employment. ☐

†   **10**   The major reason why the International Union of Official Travel
Organizations (IUOTO), a non-governmental body, was in 1975
transformed into the World Tourism Organization (WTO), an inter-
governmental body, was to

A   increase membership ☐

B   provide employment for government officials ☐

C   draw on financial contributions of governments ☐

D   influence the policies of governments in relation to tourism ☐

9.3 Organization of Tourism in the UK   UK

1 From which year dates the beginning of central government financial support for tourism in the UK?

A   1919 ☐

B   1929 ☐

C   1939 ☐

D   1949 ☐

2 Which part of the United Kingdom had no national tourism organization before 1969?

A   England ☐

B   Scotland ☐

C   Wales ☐

D   Northern Ireland ☐

3 Which of the following UK government departments is the 'sponsor ministry' for tourism

A   Education and Employment ☐

B   Environment ☐

C   National Heritage ☐

D   Trade and Industry ☐

4 Which of the following statements describes the statutory relationship between the British Tourist Authority (BTA) and the national tourist boards for England, Scotland and Wales?

A   The national boards are subordinate to BTA. ☐

B   BTA is controlled by the national boards. ☐

C   BTA controls the English Tourist Board but not the Scottish or the Wales Tourist Boards. ☐

D   They are co-equal bodies. ☐

5 Which statutory tourist board was not created under the Development of Tourism Act 1969?

A   English Tourist Board (ETB) ☐

B   Scottish Tourist Board (STB) ☐

C   Wales Tourist Board (WTB) ☐

D   Northern Ireland Tourist Board (NITB) ☐

6   Which part of the Development of Tourism Act 1969 has not been
brought into operation (by 1996)?
   A   Part I setting up four statutory tourist boards with defined
functions and powers   ☐
   B   Part II providing for financial assistance for hotel development   ☐
   C   Part III providing powers for statutory registration of tourist
accommodation (Section 17)   ☐
   D   Part III providing for statutory notification of prices of
accommodation (Section 18)   ☐

7   Which national tourist board receives the largest amount of
government grant-in-aid?
   A   English Tourist Board (ETB)   ☐
   B   Scottish Tourist Board (STB)   ☐
   C   Wales Tourist Board (WTB)   ☐
   D   Northern Ireland Tourist Board (NITB)   ☐

8   In which part of the United Kingdom has the tourism organization
below national level changed from 9 regions in 1969 to 32 areas in
1983 and to 14 areas in 1995?
   A   England   ☐
   B   Scotland   ☐
   C   Wales   ☐
   D   Northern Ireland   ☐

9   In which part of the United Kingdom has the regional tourism
framework changed from Regional Tourism Councils to Regional
Tourism Companies?
   A   England   ☐
   B   Scotland   ☐
   C   Wales   ☐
   D   Northern Ireland   ☐

10   Which of the following sources provides the largest proportion of the
income of Regional Tourist Boards in England?
   A   Commercial membership   ☐
   B   English Tourist Board (ETB)   ☐
   C   Local Authorities (LAs)   ☐
   D   Other commercial income   ☐

9.4 Tourism Organization in the UK and the Irish Republic   UK/ROI

With which parts of the United Kingdom are associated

1 Area Tourist Boards?

....

2 Regional Tourism Companies?

....

3 Regional Tourist Associations?

....

4 Regional Tourist Boards?

....

5 Tourism Development Action Plans?

....

The questions which follow refer to the Republic of Ireland.

6 Which government department is responsible for tourism?

....

7 What is the name of the national tourism organization?

....

8 How many regional tourism organizations report to the national tourism organization?

....

9 What state agency is responsible for recruitment, education and training in tourism?

....

10 What does ITIC stand for?

....

9.5 International Organizations

Which of the following are inter-governmental organizations (IGO) and which are non-governmental organizations (NGO)?

†	**1**	European Travel Commission (ETC)	....
* †	**2**	International Air Transport Association (IATA)	....
* †	**3**	International Civil Aviation Organization (ICAO)	....
†	**4**	Pacific Asia Travel Association (PATA)	....
* †	**5**	World Tourism Organization (WTO)	....

Which of the following statements apply to inter-governmental organizations (IGO) and which apply to non-governmental organizations (NGO)?

* †	**6**	Their membership consists of individuals and/or corporate bodies.	....
* †	**7**	They are created by treaties between states.	....
†	**8**	They are subject to the law of the country where their headquarters are situated.	....
†	**9**	They are subject to international law.	....
†	**10**	They are sometimes able to take decisions which are binding on their members.	....

9.6 Finance in Tourism

*† **1** Finance in tourism is influenced by the political and economic system of the country. How is an economy described in which

    A   market forces determine what is produced?

    ....

    B   the state determines what is produced?

    ....

    C   economic activities are undertaken both by private and by public enterprise?   ....

*† **2** Who normally provides infrastructure for tourism development in most countries?
    A   Private sector   ☐
    B   Public sector   ☐
    C   Voluntary sector   ☐

† **3** Infrastructure investment costs of new resort developments are sometimes recovered through
    A   levies on tour operators   ☐
    B   increased value of sites leased or sold to investors   ☐
    C   user fees levied on tourists   ☐

† **4** Which of the following organizations tend to be most capital-intensive?
    A   National Tourism Administrations   ☐
    B   Tourist Information Centres   ☐
    C   Visitor attractions   ☐

† **5** What is the main direct effect of government financial incentives for tourism development, such as grants and loans?
    A   Reduction of capital outlay   ☐
    B   Reduction of operating costs   ☐
    C   Winning investors' confidence   ☐

† **6** What is the main direct effect of government fiscal incentives for tourism development, such as 'tax holidays'?
    A   Reduction of capital outlay   ☐
    B   Reduction of operating costs   ☐
    C   Winning investors' confidence   ☐

† **7** Which of the following sources accounts for most foreign investment in tourism in developed countries?

A Foreign tour operators ☐
B International aid agencies ☐
C Private developers and investors ☐

* † **8** Which of the following functions accounts for the largest proportion of the expenditure of most tourism destination organizations?

A Industry regulation ☐
B Marketing/promotion ☐
C Research ☐

* † **9** Who provides the largest proportion of the income of the National Tourism Administration in most countries?

A Central government ☐
B Tourism industry ☐
C Tourists ☐

* † **10** What is the most common reason for governments to levy taxes on tourists?

A Allocating the social costs of tourism to users ☐
B Making tourism more acceptable to residents ☐
C Raising revenue ☐

9.7 International Sources of Finance

Below are abbreviations of ten multilateral sources of finance for tourism development. Give in full the name of each organization.

1 ADB

....

2 AFESD

....

3 CABEI

....

4 CDB

....

† **5** EBRD

....

† **6** EDF

....

† **7** EIB

....

† **8** IBRD

....

9 IDB

....

† **10** IFC

....

9.8 Abbreviations of UK Organizations UK

What do the following abbreviations stand for?

1 ABTA

....

2 BHA

....

3 CAA

....

4 HCIMA

....

5 ILAM

....

6 NITB

....

7 PSA

....

8 RMT

....

9 WDA

....

10 YHA

....

9.9 Abbreviations of US Organizations US

What do the following abbreviations stand for?

1 AAA

....

2 ABA

....

3 AH&MA

....

4 ASTA

....

5 FAA

....

6 NRA

....

7 NTA

....

8 TIA

....

9 TTRA

....

10 USTOA

....

9.10 UK versus US Financial Terms   UK/US

Give the American equivalents of the following English financial terms:

1   bank note

   ....

2   stock

   ....

3   stock turnover

   ....

4   debtors

   ....

5   creditors

   ....

6   shares

   ....

7   ordinary shares

   ....

8   preference shares

   ....

9   wages and salaries

   ....

10   capital gearing

   ....

Part Ten
Miscellaneous Topics

10.1 Countries and Currencies

What are the currencies of the following countries?

* †   **1**   Austria

....

* †   **2**   Denmark

....

* †   **3**   Germany

....

* †   **4**   Hong Kong

....

* †   **5**   India

....

* †   **6**   Italy

....

* †   **7**   Netherlands

....

* †   **8**   Poland

....

* †   **9**   Portugal

....

* †   **10**   Spain

....

10.2 Currencies and Countries

Which countries have the following currencies?

* † **1** Drachma

....

* † **2** Florin (Fl)

....

3 Koruna (Kč/Ks)

....

4 Markka (Mk)

....

5 Naira (₦)

....

* † **6** Rand (R)

....

* † **7** Rouble/Rubl/Ruble (R)

....

8 Tolar (Slt)

....

9 Won

....

* † **10** Yen

....

10.3 Employment Terms

What term describes

* † **1** employment on one's own account, with or without any employees?

....

* † **2** working in one or more jobs in addition to one's normal employment?

....

* † **3** economic activities not declared for taxation purposes?

....

† **4** not declaring one's employment for taxation purposes?

....

† **5** working from home using information technology?

....

What term describes an employment arrangement under which

† **6** a person is employed by the hour or on a day-to-day basis?

....

† **7** each employee can choose within limits his/her working hours?

....

† **8** a full-time job is performed by more than one person each working part-time?

....

* † **9** two working periods separated by a long interval?

....

* † **10** the total number of hours over which work extends in a day exceeds the number of hours worked?

....

10.4 Nautical Terms

Give the nautical terms for the following:

* † **1** rear of a ship

....

* † **2** front of a ship

....

* † **3** middle part of a ship

....

* † **4** left side of a ship

....

* † **5** right side of a ship

....

6 sheltered side of a ship (against wind)

....

7 least sheltered side of a ship (against wind)

....

8 depth of the bottom of a ship below the water surface

....

9 breadth of a ship at its widest point

....

10 at right angles to the length of a ship

....

10.5 Food and Catering Terms

What term describes the following?

* †   **1**   Food fulfilling requirements of Jewish law

....

†   **2**   Food fulfilling requirements of Muslim law

....

* †   **3**   Food partially or fully prepared by the manufacturer and used as labour-saving alternative to raw food

....

* †   **4**   Limited choice menu with a single price for any combination of items chosen or with a price determined by the choice of the main dish

....

* †   **5**   Menu providing a choice of items, each of which is priced separately

....

* †   **6**   Meal served between normal breakfast and lunch times and replacing breakfast and lunch

....

†   **7**   Style of restaurant table service in which food is portioned and plated in the kitchen

....

†   **8**   Trolley from which final preparation and service of a dish is performed in a restaurant

....

†   **9**   Style of restaurant table service in which portioned food is served from silver salvers placed on a gueridon

....

† **10** Place where a number of different food outlets share a common eating area

....

10.6 Airlines and Hotels, 1945–1995

At various times since the end of World War II airlines have owned hotels. The first column below lists ten such airlines and the second column the hotel companies which were or still are owned by them. Show in the space below the hotel company owned by each of the airlines.

1	Aer Lingus	**A**	Ana Enterprises
2	Air France	**B**	Copthorne Hotels
3	Air India	**C**	Sunwing Hotels
4	All Nippon Airways	**D**	Hilton International
5	Japan Airlines	**E**	Hotel Corporation of India
6	Pan American	**F**	Inter-Continental Hotels
7	SAS	**G**	Meridien Hotels
8	TWA	**H**	Nikko Hotels International
9	United Airlines	**I**	Tropical Hotels
10	VARIG	**J**	Westin Hotels

Airline	1	2	3	4	5	6	7	8	9	10
Hotel co.										

10.7 Tourism and Technology

What term describes

† **1** the first system for high speed electronic transmission of an exact copy of a document between locations?

† **2** electronic services which display transmitted information on a video screen?

† **3** an electronic communication system in which money is transferred between accounts through terminals in retail outlets and computers in banks?

† **4** a system in which cards issued by airlines enable passengers to obtain a boarding card from a machine at the airport?

† **5** computer simulation which attempts to replace the user's experience of the physical world with three-dimensional effects?

Which computer reservation system (CRS)

6 is owned jointly by Air France, Iberia and Lufthansa?

7 is owned in part by QANTAS?

8 is owned by American Airlines?

9 was formed as a joint venture between DATAS II and PARS systems in 1990?

10 merged with the Galileo network to form Galileo International in 1992?

10.8 US versus UK Language   US/UK

Give the English equivalents of the following American terms:

1 bed and board

....

2 bypass

....

3 cutting in line

....

4 in-plant travel agency

....

5 interval ownership

....

6 one-way ticket

....

7 slip

....

8 subway

....

9 truck shop

....

10 ZIP code

....

10.9 UK Leaders in the Tourism Industry
UK

In the UK, which

1 is the largest airline?

....

2 airport handles the most passengers?

....

3 is the longest pleasure pier?

....

4 is the largest charter airline?

....

5 is the largest cross-Channel ferry operator?

....

6 is the biggest hotel?

....

7 hotel company has the largest market share?

....

8 tour operator has the largest market share?

....

9 travel agency has the most retail outlets?

....

10 attraction has the largest number of visitors?

....

10.10 World Leaders in the Tourism Industry

Which is the world's

1 largest airline?

....

2 busiest airport?

....

3 biggest passenger ship?

....

4 biggest hotel?

....

5 airport handling most international passengers?

....

6 largest restaurant company?

....

7 largest shopping complex?

....

8 largest employer?

....

9 biggest sea ferry?

....

10 attraction with most visitors?

....

Answers

Part 1
Anatomy of Tourism

1.1 Defining Tourism and Tourists

1 D F.W. Ogilvie (in *The Tourist Movement*, Staples Press, 1933; *The Tourist Industry* was published by Pitman in 1936, *Allgemeine Fremdenverkehrslehre* by Polygraphischer Verlag, Zurich in 1942, *The Travel Trade* by Practical Press in 1958)

2 A staying
  B environment   See World Tourism Organization (1993),
  C not more   *Recommendations on Tourism Statistics*,
  D business   Madrid: WTO

3 AB Technical definitions are used in both.

4 C Purpose of trip (which distinguishes between tourism and other travel and between particular forms of tourism)

5 A tourists   Leiper, N. (1979) The Framework of Tourism:
  B regions   Towards a Definition of Tourism,
  C destination   Tourist, and the Tourist Industry,
  D tourist   *Annals of Tourism Research*, 6(4), 390–407

6 D Much tourism involves discretionary use of time and money. (See Question 2 above.)

7 D Domestic tourism is not better documented.

8 A Air crews staying overnight at the destination (See WTO, *Recommendations on Tourism Statistics*)

9 A Diplomats travelling between their country of origin and duty station (as above).

10

1st column	1	2	3
2nd column	C	B	A

1.2 Studying Tourism

1	Economics
2	Geography
3	Psychology
4	Politics
5	Sociology
6	Balneology
7	Ecology
8	Demography
9	Meteorology
10	Topography

1.3 Types and Forms of Tourism

1   D   visits with a purpose significantly shared by the visitor and visited (including B and C but not confined to them)

2   C   trips and visits motivated by cultural interests

3   C   travel within one's own country

4   D   visits for ethnic reunion (also visits to places inhabited by indigenous and other exotic people)

5   C   visits to health resorts and establishments

6   B   travel paid for by a firm as a reward to employees (also, e.g., to dealers and agents and often including spouses)

7   A   most travel between countries

8   A   tourism in which large numbers take part

9   C   travel to countryside destinations

10   C   travel to town and city destinations

1.4 Propensities, Determinants, Motivations

1   A $\text{Net propensity} = 60\% \left(\dfrac{33 \text{ million}}{55 \text{ million}} \right) \times 100$

     B $\text{Gross propensity} = 80\% \left(\dfrac{44 \text{ million}}{55 \text{ million}} \right) \times 100$

     C $\text{Frequency} = 1.33 \left(\dfrac{44 \text{ million}}{33 \text{ million}} \right)$

2 C Standard of living (commonly measured by GDP/GNP per capita)
3 D level of education
4 A Supply/determinant
   B Demand determinant
   C Supply determinant
   D Demand determinant
5 C decrease arrivals from other countries
6 A migration
7 C Human needs as motivators form a hierarchy.
8 A allocentric
   B psychocentric
9 A Wanderlust ⎫ Gray, H.P. (1970) *International Travel –*
   B Wanderlust ⎬ *International Trade*, Lexington: Heath
   C Sunlust   ⎪ Lexington Books
   D Sunlust   ⎭
10 D It refers to purchases which satisfy a psychological need. (See Veblen, T. (1899) *The Theory of the Leisure Class*, New York: Mentor, 1953)

1.5 Describing People

1   citizen/national
2   emigrant
3   expatriate
4   exile/refugee
5   tourist/overnight visitor/stayover visitor
6   (same) day visitor/excursionist
7   alien
8   guest worker
9   nomad
10 commuter

1.6 Tourism Concepts

1 A common interest tourism
2 A destination
3 B disposable income
4 B internal tourism
5 B national tourism
6 B rural tourism
7 A health tourism

8	A	leisure
9	B	visitor
10	A	traveller

1.7 Tourism Synonyms

1	national
2	(same) day visitor
3	advanced/developed countries
4	inclusive tour
5	domicile
6	alternative/appropriate/green/soft tourism
7	tertiary industries
8	developing/less developed/underdeveloped countries
9	(tour) wholesaler
10	tourism industry

1.8 Tourism Opposites

1	leisure/pleasure/private/holiday (vacation) travel
2	international tourism
3	immigrant
4	individual travel
5	outbound tourism
6	independent tour
7	additional holiday (vacation)
8	(same) day visit
9	tourist destination area
10	rural tourism

1.9 US versus UK Language

1	car hire
2	(motor) car
3	camping site
4	hotel industry
5	(motor) caravan
6	price/rate increase/rise
7	railway

8 holiday
9 holiday/second home
10 holiday trip

1.10 The Language North of the Border

1 glen
2 strath
3 kyle/sound
4 loch
5 Ben
6 Munro
7 mull
8 firth
9 brig
10 bothie/bothy

Part 2
Historical Development of Tourism

2.1 Worldwide Development

1	C	confined to a small fraction of the population
2	C	increased urbanization
3	D	increase in employment (directly and indirectly)
4	B	to enable steamers to land
5	D	to transport money and valuables
6	D	originating the inclusive tour
7	C	to shorten maritime routes between Europe and the Orient (previously round the Cape of Good Hope)
8	D	to safeguard their passenger traffic
9	D	stimulus to visiting friends and relatives
10	C	growth in air transport

2.2 British Development I

1	C	business and vocational reasons
2	A	Bath
3	B	18th century
4	C	Brighton
5	B	18th century
6	B	1840s (more miles of track opened than during any other decade)
7	C	ensure a minimum holiday entitlement for all
8	C	Train (with more than one billion passengers per annum)
9	B	1918–1938 (more passengers carried than before or after)
10	A	1936 (by Butlin at Skegness)

2.3 British Development II

1 B 1 First stage coach services (mid-17th century)
 C 2 First railway construction (early 19th century)
 A 3 Beginnings of the motor car (late 19th century)
2 C 1 Inns (early Middle Ages)
 B 2 Hotels (first family hotel in Covent Garden 1774)
 A 3 Motels (first Graham Lyon motel at Hythe, Kent, 1953)
3 C 1 First major excursion to London (to Great Exhibition 1851)
 B 2 First hotel coupon (1867)
 A 3 First round-the-world tour (1872)
4 C 1 National Trust (1895)
 B 2 First Town and Country Planning Act (1947)
 A 3 Countryside Commission (1968)
5 B 1 Scottish Travel Association (1930)
 C 2 Wales Tourist and Holidays Board (1948)
 A 3 English Tourist Board (1969)
6 C 1 Olympic Games (1948)
 B 2 Festival of Britain (1951)
 A 3 Coronation of Queen Elizabeth II (1953)
7 C 1 Westbury (1955)
 B 2 Skyway (1960)
 A 3 London Hilton (1963)
8 C 1 Prestige Hotels (1966)
 B 2 Interchange Hotels (1968)
 A 3 Inter Hotels (1969)
9 C 1 First motorway, M1 (1959)
 B 2 Advanced Passenger Train (1984)
 A 3 Channel Tunnel (1994)
10 B 1 Gatwick Airport (1958)
 A 2 London City Airport (1987)
 C 3 Stansted Airport (1991)

2.4 American Development

1 B 1830 (the Baltimore & Ohio Railroad, followed by the Boston & Maine Railroad, and then the Charleston & Hamburg (South Carolina) Railroad, all in the same year)
2 B 1850 (by the merger of Wells & Co., founded 1844, Livingston, Fargo & Co. and Wasson & Co., founded 1849)

3	B	1872 (as the first National Park anywhere, by the Yellowstone National Park Act; the Rocky Mountain Parks Act of 1887 established the first Canadian National Park surrounding Banff, Alberta)
4	C	1925 (by Varney Air Lines from Pasco, Washington, to Boise, Idaho and then Elko, Nevada)
5	C	1925 (Vail's Motor Inn at San Luis Obispo, California, is credited as being the first)
6	B	1930s (completed in 1936)
7	B	1954
8	B	1955
9	B	1978 (with the Airline Deregulation Act of that year)
10	C	1994

2.5 Transport Development

1	A	1830 (between Liverpool and Manchester, England)
2	B	1840 (by Cunard)
3	B	1869
4	A	1919 (first by the UK Air Ministry to carry members of the government to the Peace Conference, followed in the same year by two private companies)
5	B	1939 (by Imperial Airways and Pan American)
6	B	1957
7	B	1952
8	B	1957
9	B	1977
10	B	1976

2.6 World Events since 1945

1	1948
2	1950
3	1956
4	1956
5	1967
6	1968
7	1968
8	1982
9	1991
10	1991

2.7 World Tourism since 1945

1	1945 (in Havana, Cuba)
2	1946 (renegotiated as Bermuda Two in 1977)
3	1948
4	1958 (by Boeing 707 Paris–New York and Comet 4 London–New York)
5	1963 (in Rome)
6	1967 (designated as such by the United Nations)
7	1975
8	1990 (under the auspices of the European Commission)
9	1992 (when international tourism receipts exceeded US$ 300 billion for the first time)
10	1994

2.8 Who Was Who in Tourism Worldwide

1	Mark Twain (1835–1910), US writer, journalist, lecturer
2	Sir Samuel Cunard (1787–1865), shipowner born in Canada, emigrated to England, co-founder of Cunard Line
3	Karl Baedeker (1801–59), German publisher
4	George Mortimer Pullman (1831–97), US inventor, designer, businessman
5	Henry Wells (1805–78), US shipper specializing in valuables and bullion
6	Sir Henry Lunn (1859–1939), British skiing pioneer
7	César Ritz (1850–1918), Swiss-born hotelier
8	Ellsworth Milton Statler (1863–1928), US hotelier
9	Walt Disney (1901–66), US film producer
10	Sir Freddie Laker (1922–), British entrepreneur

2.9 Who Was Who in British Tourism

1	John Metcalf (1717–1810), Scottish engineer and one of the great road-makers of the 18th century
2	Dr Richard Russell (died 1771), with his treatise on the use of sea water in the treatment of diseases (1752)
3	(Richard) Beau Nash (1674–1762), best known for his brilliant organization of social life at Bath

4   Isambard Kingdom Brunel (1806–59), British engineer who built steam-powered ships, railways and bridges

5   Thomas Cook (1808–92), tour operator, retail travel agent and publisher

6   John Murray (1808–92), famous for his red handbooks

7   Sir John Lubbock (1834–1913), banker, created Baron Avebury 1910

8   Arnold Bennett (1867–1931), whose novel was based on the Savoy Hotel in London

9   William (Billy) Butlin (1899–1980), South African-born, funfair and holiday camp promoter

10   Lord (then Dr Richard) Beeching (1913–85), known for rationalization of rail services, stations and lines as chairman of British Railways (1962–5)

2.10 British Prime Ministers and Tourism

1   Harold Macmillan (1957–63)

2   Clement Atlee (1945–51)

3   James Callaghan (1976–9)

4   Harold Wilson (1964–6, 1966–70, 1974–6)

5   Edward Heath (1970–4)

6   Harold Wilson (1964–6, 1966–70, 1974–6)

7   Edward Heath (1970–4)

8   Harold Wilson (1964–6, 1966–70, 1974–6)

9   Harold Macmillan (1957–63)

10   Margaret Thatcher (1979–90)

Part 3
Geography of Tourism

3.1 Introducing Geography of Tourism

1	Spain and Portugal
2	Norway and Sweden
3	Nairobi, Kenya
4	Nadi, Fiji
5	Jerusalem
6	Mecca
7	Three (cold, hot, wet)
8	Two (winter and summer)
9	lose
10	gain

3.2 Country Groupings

1	Scandinavia
2	Nordic countries
3	Melanesia
4	Second World
5	First World
6	Old World
7	New World
8	Pacific Rim countries
9	Gulf States
10	Latin America

3.3 World's Coastal Resorts

1   Mexico
2   France
3   Croatia
4   Israel
5   Spain
6   Kenya
7   Jamaica
8   Italy
9   USA (California)
10   Netherlands

3.4 World's Inland Resorts

1   USA (Colorado)
2   Germany (formerly West Germany)
3   Canada (Alberta)
4   France
5   Switzerland
6   Czech Republic (formerly Czechoslovakia)
7   Norway
8   Italy
9   India
10   Austria

3.5 World's National Parks

1   Nepal
2   Australia
3   Indonesia
4   New Zealand
5   England
6   Croatia
7   Tanzania
8   Guatemala
9   Canada (NW Territories/Alberta)
10   USA (California)

3.6 World's Heritage Attractions

1   Greece
2   Brazil
3   Italy
4   Spain
5   China
6   England
7   France
8   Jordan
9   USA (New Jersey)
10 India

3.7 Names and By-names of Countries, Regions and Places

1   Aruba, Bonaire, Curacao
2   African, Caribbean, Pacific States (under Lomé Conventions)
3   Lithuania, Latvia, Estonia
4   Belgium, Holland, Luxembourg
5   Denmark, Finland, Iceland, Norway, Sweden
6   Tasmania, Australia
7   New York, USA
8   California, USA
9   Quebec
10 Zanzibar

3.8 British Islands and Tourist Regions

1   Isle of Man
2   Isle of Wight
3   Scilly Isles
4   Channel Islands
5   Shetland
6   East Anglia
7   Heart of England
8   Northumbria
9   Cumbria
10 West Country

3.9 Scales and Instruments

1	Millibar
2	Richter
3	Beaufort
4	Celsius/centigrade
5	Fahrenheit
6	Altimeter
7	Barometer
8	Hygrometer/wet-bulb thermometer
9	Anemometer (a wind sock gives an indication)
10	Pedometer

3.10 Abbreviations of Countries, Regions and Places

1	British Virgin Islands
2	European Union
3	Federal Republic of Germany
4	Isle of Man
5	Latin America/Los Angeles/Louisiana
6	Maine/Middle East
7	New Zealand
8	Papua New Guinea
9	People's Republic China
10	West Indies/Wisconsin

Part 4
Dimensions of Tourism

4.1 Framework of Tourism Statistics

1	residents
2	non-residents
3	residents
4	inbound
5	outbound
6	outbound
7	visitors
8	tourists
9	twelve
10	remunerated

4.2 Basic Tourism Statistics

1	same-day
2	Total days/nights
3	Total visits
4	Total expenditure
5	Total days/nights
6	profile
7	behaviour
8	profile
9	profile
10	behaviour

4.3 Definitions, Scope and Sources of Tourism Statistics

1 C at least one night
2 D a survey of departing (returning) visitors
3 D country of residence
4 C transport used by a visitor to travel from his/her place of usual residence to places visited
5 B Fare payments for international transport
6 C sample surveys of visitors
7 C They measure numbers of visits, not visitors
8 A The number of visits to a destination is *not* the best indication of the value of tourism to the destination.
9 A Delphi
10

1st column	1	2	3
2nd column	C	B	A

4.4 Patterns of International Tourism

1 C 500–600 million (566 million in 1995)
2 B Holiday (vacation) (around 60% of the world total)
3 A between developed countries (around 60% of the world total)
4 D within Europe (around 50% of the world total)
5 D Europe (around 60% of arrivals and 50% of receipts in mid-1990s)
6 C East Asia and Pacific (average 13.5% p.a. arrivals and 16.4% p.a. receipts between 1984 and 1994)
7 A France (60.1 million, Spain 39.3 million, USA 43.4 million, Italy 31.1 million in 1995)
8 D USA (US$61.1bn, France US$27.5bn, Italy US$27.5bn, Spain US$25.3bn)
9 D USA (50.8 million in 1995)
10 D USA (US$60.2m in 1995)

4.5 Tourism-related Surveys in the UK

1   Day Visits Survey (DVS)
2   United Kingdom Tourism Survey (UKTS)
3   Labour Force Survey (LFS)
4   Family Expenditure Survey (FES)
5   British National Travel Survey (BNTS)
6   International Passenger Survey (IPS)
7   National Travel Survey (NTS)
8   National Readership Survey (NRS)
9   United Kingdom Tourism Survey (UKTS)
10   International Passenger Survey (IPS)

4.6 UK Tourism in Figures

1   A   100 million + (121 million in 1995)
2   A   4 nights (1993: 4.1, 1994: 3.8, 1995: 3.7 nights)
3   A   much larger (64% compared with 36% in 1995)
4   C   West Country (16% trips, 21% nights, 22% spending in 1995)
5   B   Holiday (vacation) (55%, VFR 29%, business 12% in 1995)
6   A   Scotland (7%, Wales 5%, Northern Ireland 1% of total in 1995)
7   B   Car (75% trips, bus/coach 9%, train 9% in 1995)
8   A   Friends'/relatives' home (42% nights, self-catering 26%, serviced 20% in 1995)
9   A   Accommodation (1995 survey: 37%, eating out 24%, travel 17%)
10   B   Towns (43%, seaside 36%, countryside 21% in 1995)

4.7 UK in International Tourism

1   B   20–30 million (24.0 million in 1995)
2   C   USA (1995: 3.3 million, France 3.2 million, Germany 2.7 million)
3   A   Air (1995: 68%, sea 25%, Channel Tunnel 7%)
4   B   Holiday (vacation) (1995: 44%, business 25%, visiting friends or relatives 19%, miscellaneous 12%)
5   B   10–20% (13.6% in 1995)
6   B   35–45 million (41.9 million in 1995)
7   A   France (1995: 9.7 million, Spain 8.3 million, USA 2.7 million; actually the Irish Republic ranked third, with 2.8 million in 1995)
8   A   Air (1995: 68%, sea 27%, Channel Tunnel 5%)

9   B   Holiday (vacation) (1995: 67%, business 15%, visiting friends or relatives 12%, miscellaneous 6%)

10   B   Between 30% and 50% (36.6% in 1995)

4.8   USA in International Tourism

1   B   40–50 million (43.4 million in 1995)
2   C   Overseas (1995: 47.6%, Canada 33.8%, Mexico 18.6%)
3   B   Japan (1995: 4.6 million, UK 2.9 million, Germany 1.8 million)
4   B   Brazil (1995: 838,000, Venezuela 511,000, Argentina 383,000)
5   C   Overseas (+ 12% in 1995, decline from Canada and Mexico)
6   B   5–10% (7.6% in 1995)
7   B   Florida (1994: US$12.0bn, California $11.5bn, New York $7.6bn)
8   A   It is larger (e.g., 50.8 million compared to 43.4 million in 1995)
9   C   Overseas (1995: 38%, Mexico 36%, Canada 26%)
10   A   Positive throughout the 1990s (e.g., US$19.5bn in 1995)

4.9   Australia in International Tourism

1   B   Inbound tourism (between 1985 and 1995 international visitor arrivals increased by an average of 13% p.a., well above the rate of growth of domestic and outbound tourism)
2   B   3–4 million (3.7 million in 1995 but more than 4 million in 1996)
3   B   20–30 nights (21 nights in 1995 and declining)
4   A   Asia (51%, Europe 20%, North America 10% in 1995)
5   A   Japan (21%, New Zealand 14%, UK 9% in 1995)
6   B   Leisure, recreation and holidays (63%, other 22%, business and professional 15% in 1994)
7   A   Air (over 99%)
8   B   10–15% (12.7% of current account credits in 1995)
9   B   2–3 million (2.5 million in 1995)
10   A   increased significantly (1985: 1.5 million, 1995: 2.5 million)

4.10 The Caribbean in International Tourism

1   A   Cuba (11.0 million, Dominican Republic 8.0 million, Haiti 7.0 million in 1995)
2   B   Dominican Republic (32,000 rooms; Cuba 24,000; Jamaica 21,000 rooms in 1995)

3 B 10–15 million (14.7 million in 1995)
4 A faster (on average 8.4% p.a. compared with 7.2% p.a.)
5 C US Territories (3.6 million, Dutch West Indies 1.4 million, French West Indies 1.1 million in 1995)
6 C Puerto Rico (3.1 million, Dominican Republic 1.9 million, Jamaica 1.1 million in 1995)
7 C USA (over 50%, Europe approx. 20%, Caribbean less than 10% of the total in 1995)
8 B Around 10 million (9.7 million in 1995)
9 A Bahamas (1.5 million, US Virgin Islands 1.2 million, Puerto Rico 1.0 million in 1995)
10 C Puerto Rico (US$1.8 bn, Dominican Republic US$1.6 bn, Bahamas US$1.3 bn)

Part 5
Significance of Tourism

5.1   Economic Aspects of Tourism

1   A   Economic aspects
2   C   None
3   A   It is a relatively free market.
4   C   Volatile demand and fixed supply
5   C   Monopolistic competition
6   A   They are perishable.
7   A   Holidays (vacations)
8   B   Additional (secondary) holidays (vacations)
9   C   Travel agencies
10 B   Resort condominia (they are normally owned – interior units individually, land and buildings in common)

5.2   Economic Impacts of Tourism

1   B   more people are employed in the tertiary sector
2   A   Leakages
    B   Induced
    C   Indirect
    D   Secondary
3   A   Indirect
    B   Indirect
    C   Direct
    D   Direct
4 C1   Souvenir shops
  D2   Taxis
  A3   Banks
  B4   Public utilities
5   C   Tourism spending to GDP or GNP
6   A   Credits

B   Debits
C   Credits
D   Debits
7   C   High indigenous ownership of tourism industry
8   A   As long as demand exists for locally produced goods and services, each successive round of spending generates new income.
9   A   Low diversification of the economy
10   1,250

5.3   Social Aspects and Impacts of Tourism

1   B   Businessmen
2   B   acculturation (also described as accommodation/assimilation)
3   D   ethnocentricism
4   C   demonstration effect
5   D   xenophobia
6 C1   euphoria
  B2   apathy   In *Heritage Canada*, Vol. 2, 1976, pp. 26–7
  D3   irritation
  A4   antagonism
7   D   assisted holidays (vacations) for disadvantaged groups in society
8   D   None of these
9   B   Tourism can be a lever for social change.
10   A   No (*The Golden Hordes*, London: Constable)
     B   No (*The Tourist*, London: Macmillan)
     C   Yes (*The Restless Generation*, London: Davis-Poynter)
     D   Yes (*Tourism – Passport to Development?* Oxford: OUP)

5.4   Environmental Aspects and Impacts of Tourism

1

Aspect of environment	1	2	3	4
Part of world	D	A	B	C

2

Type of pollution	1	2	3	4		1	2
Main cause	B	A	D	C		A	B

also acceptable

3

Problem	1	2	3	4
Type of location	C	D	A	B

4

Issue	1	2	3	4
Effect	C	D	A	B

5 A environmental audit
   B alternative/appropriate/responsible/soft tourism
   C global warming
   D renewable resources

6

Explanation	1	2	3	4
Term	C	D	A	B

7 A Alternative/appropriate/green/responsible/soft tourism
   B Appropriate/responsible tourism
   C Ecotourism/green tourism
   D Green holidays (vacations)
8 A Coach (0.023 lb per passenger mile, train 0.073 lb, medium car 0.180 lb, jumbo jet 0.347 lb, *Aeronautical Journal*, Vol. 78, No. 765, 1974)
9 D Hang gliding
10 A European Prize for Tourism and the Environment
    B Blue Flag

5.5 Measures of Tourism Distribution and Impacts

1 Tourist intensity index (D.E. Lundberg, 1974)
2 Tourist function index (P. Defert, 1967)
3 Ratio index (M. Jensen-Verbeke, 1995)
4 Concentration index (M. Jensen-Verbeke, 1995)
5 Trip index (D.G. Pearce and J.M. Elliott, 1995)
6 Connectivity index (S.L.J. Smith, 1989)
7 Compactness index (W.J. Coffey, 1981)
8 Directional bias index (R.I. Wolfe, 1966)
9 Peaking index (D.J. Stynes, 1978)
10 Tourism attractiveness index (G.E. Gearing, W.W. Swart and T. Var, 1974)

See the following sources for details:

Q1   Lundberg, D.E. (1974) *The Tourist Business*, 2nd edn, Boston, MA: Cahners

Q2   Smith, S.L.J. (1989) *Tourism Analysis: A Handbook*, London: Longman

Q3, 4 *Tourism Management*, Vol. 16, No. 1, February 1995

Q5   *Journal of Travel Research*, Vol. 32, No. 1, 1995: 6–9

Q6–10 Smith, S.L.J. (1989), as above

5.6   Developed Countries and Tourism

1   B   Walt Whitman Rostow (1959), US economic historian (1916–)
2   A   Gross national product (GNP) per capita
3   C   Large tertiary sector
4   B   They are not important tourist destinations.
5   C   Spain
6   A   Around 1%
7   B   Around 2%
8   A   Around 5%
9   A   Around 5%
10 A   Around 7%

5.7   Developing Countries and Tourism

1   A   Brandt Commission (Independent Commission on International Development Issues set up in 1977 at the suggestion of the President of the World Bank under the Chairmanship of Willy Brandt, German statesman and Nobel Peace Prize winner in 1971)
2   C   They are short of capital
3   C   Most developing countries (do not) generate more tourism than they receive
4   B   Israel
5   B   earns foreign currency
6   B   Faster
7   B   One-quarter
8   B   They are lower
9   A   Mexico (1995: 20.0m, Singapore 6.6m, Thailand 6.5m)
10 B   Singapore (1995: US$ 7,550m, Thailand US$ 6,617m, Mexico US$ 6,070m.

5.8 Tourism and the UK Economy

1	B	Around 4%: 1993: 3.8%, 1994: 3.8%, 1995: 4.0%
2	B	Around 5%: 1993: 4.6%, 1994: 4.8%, 1995: 5.1% (Provisional)
3	B	Around 30%: 1993: 30.4%, 1994: 30.1%, 1995: 33.4% (Provisional)
4	B	Around 6%: 1993: 6.0%, 1994: 6.0%, 1995: 6.2% (Provisional)
5	C	Tourism (1995: £12.1 m, petroleum products £8.7 m, textiles £3.3 m)
6	A	Hotels and other accommodation (1992 survey: 36.1%, retailing 24.5%, travel within UK 8.0%)
7	A	Hotels and other accommodation (1995 survey: 37.0%, eating out 24.0%, travel within UK 17.0%)
8	A	Catering (1992 survey: meals, snacks, alcoholic and non-alcoholic drinks 38%; gifts, souvenirs, clothes 22%; fuel, fares, parking charges 18%)
9	C	Around 1.5 million
10	A	Another half-a-job

5.9 Tourism and the US Economy

1	B	Around 6%
2	C	Around 10%
3	B	Food service
4	A 1	Automotive dealers
	B 2	Food stores
	C 3	Travel and tourism
5	B	Between 2 and 3 (2.4)
6	B	Between 6 and 8 million (6.6 million in 1995)
7	A	Around 5%
8	B	2–3 times (2.4 times including indirect and induced effects)
9	C	4–5% (4.3% in 1995)
10	C	South Atlantic

5.10 International Organizations

1	Association of South East Asian Nations
2	International Labour Organisation
3	Organization for Economic Cooperation and Development
4	Third World European Ecumenical Network
5	United Nations Conference on Trade and Development

6	United Nations Development Programme
7	United Nations Environmental Programme
8	United Nations Educational, Scientific and Cultural Organization
9	World Tourism Organization
10	World Travel and Tourism Council

Part 6
The Tourism Industry

6.1   Tourism as an Industry

1   A   Establishments (firms and occupations may cut across industries)
2   C   To promote uniformity and comparability of official statistics
3   C   It is synonymous with tourism supply.
4   C   Tourism-related industries (do not) serve only tourists.
5   A   activities
    B   services
    C   foreign
6   B   Conference centre ownership and management
7   C   Product perishability
8   A   Hotels and catering
9   B   mainly from other industries into tourism industry
10 A   Lateral/horizontal
    B   Vertical backward
    C   Vertical forward

6.2   Visitor Attractions Worldwide

1   A   environment
    B   choice
    C   motivation
2   C   The visitor experience
3   B   Distance from concentrations of population
4   A   Motivator
    B   Motivator
    C   Determinant
5   A   Heritage sites/historic buildings
    B   Ancient monuments
    C   Industrial archaeology/heritage
6   A   Admission charges

7 B Payroll
8 A Total visitors
   B Income
9 A Site (Valley of the Kings)
   B Event (Passion Play)
   C Site (Disneyworld)
10 A National
   B International
   C Regional

6.3   Visitor Attractions in Britain

1   Public sector
2   Voluntary sector
3   Regional
4   National
5   'Time cars'
6   Canal boats
7   Lake District (2,280 sq. km)
8   North Yorkshire Moors (438 sq. km)
9   St Kilda
10 Gwynedd (castles and town walls dating from the reign of Edward I)

6.4   Transport Modes

1   Coach
2   Motor car/taxi
3   Germany
4   Italy
5   Japan
6   France
7   Catamaran
8   Hydrofoil
9   Road
10 Air

6.5   Air Transport

1	C	High fixed costs (also most other transport modes)
2	B	Load tonne-kilometres and capacity tonne-kilometres
3	C	One who breaks a journey at an intermediate point
4	B	Charter flights have higher load factors than scheduled flights.
5	B	Codes denoting cities/airports
6	C	Warsaw Convention (1929 with subsequent amendments)
7	C	Traffic rights (Third, Fourth and Fifth freedoms)
8	A	Los Angeles – Honolulu
9	C	growth in air transport
10	C	British European Airways (BEA) and British Overseas Airways Corporation (BOAC) (1973)

6.6   Transport Synonyms and Opposites

1	return load
2	cabin baggage/hand luggage
3	stopover
4	International Load Line
5	aft/abaft
6	bow/forward
7	scheduled airline
8	port
9	air transport
10	through passenger

6.7   Hotels and Other Tourism Accommodation

1	C	High investment intensity (90% or more in fixed assets)
2	A	Bed occupancy
	B	Room occupancy
	C	Average room rate
3	B	Building (commonly 70–80% of total investment)
4	C	Payroll (commonly 30–40% of sales)
5	A	Hotel room occupancies are normally higher than bed occupancies
6	B	It (does not) determine most tourists' choice of destinations

7 C1 Hotels
A2 Motels
B3 Camping sites
8 B hotel classification
9

Accommodation	1	2	3
Users	B	C	A

10 C Hospitality Franchise Systems

6.8 Accommodation Types and Tariffs

1 New Zealand (North Island; called a crib in South Island)
2 France
3 Spain
4 Portugal
5 Japan
6 European Plan (EP)
7 Continental Plan (CP)
8 Bermuda Plan (BP)
9 Modified American Plan (MAP)
10 American Plan (AP)

6.9 Tour Operations and Travel Agencies

1 C Obtaining travel insurance
2 C Travel insurance (typically 30% or more)
3 C Payroll (typically around 50% or more)
4 C The longer the distance, the higher the tour operator's profit
5 B They accommodate inclusive tours on both scheduled and charter flights
6 D Inclusive tours
7 A Airlines
8 D United States
9 D United States
10 A Germany

6.10 Travel Trade Abbreviations

1	Advance Booking Charter
2	Bank Settlement Plan
3	domestic escorted tour
4	domestic independent tour
5	foreign escorted tour
6	foreign independent tour
7	group inclusive tour
8	General Sales Agent
9	inclusive tour
10	inclusive tour charter

Part 7
Marketing in Tourism

7.1   The Marketing Concept

1	A	target	Kotler, P. (1991) *Marketing Management: Analysis,*
	B	satisfactions	*Planning and Control*, 7th edn, Englewood Cliffs,
	C	competitors	NJ: Prentice Hall
2	A	satisfaction	
	B	identifiable	Krippendorf, J. (1971) *Marketing et Tourisme,*
	C	appropriate	Berne: Lang
3	A	production	
	B	sales	
	C	marketing	

4   A   Marketing is about consumer orientation
5   B   Actual or potential demand for a product
6   A   They are composite products
7   B   They are a major determinant of tourists' choice of destinations
8   B   They are bought by tourists individually or as part of a package
9   C   It is interpreted in terms of the time taken and/or the cost involved to reach a destination
10 C   destination organizations and individual operators

7.2   Marketing Tools

1   B   the marketing mix
2   C   homogeneous groups
3   B   Life style
4   A   Beach holidays (vacations) in Greece and in Turkey
5   C   a regular repeat survey which covers a number of topics for different clients
6   B   Products are shaped to match markets
7   B   Attractions (climate controlled)
8   B   conveying signs, concepts and images

9 A   Intermediaries
     B   Principals
     C   Principals
     D   Intermediaries
10 D   Their geographical distribution tends to reflect market density

7.3 Tourism Promotion

1 B   The promoter has no control over the message
2 B   The advertiser buys space or time in the media
3 C   Their function is to attract the potential customer to the point of sale
4 C   It is below-the-line promotion
5 B   It seeks to influence potential customers at the point of sale
6 B   they act as a product substitute at the point of sale
7 B   the number of sold copies
8 B   the ratio of customers who buy a product to the number of responses received to an advertisement
9 B   The media
10 C   Tourist board publicity in a generating country

7.4 Pricing Methods and Approaches

1   Backward pricing
2   Cost-plus pricing
3   Differential pricing/price discrimination
4   Marginal cost pricing
5   Predatory pricing
6   Price cutting
7   Price pegging
8   Price skimming
9   Rate-of-return pricing
10 Resale price maintenance

7.5 Pricing Hotel and Transport Services

1   American Plan
2   Advance Purchase Excursion Fare
3   Bermuda Plan
4   Continental Plan

5	European Plan
6	Group Inclusive Tour Fare
7	Instant Purchase Excursion Fare
8	Inclusive Tour Fare
9	Modified American Plan
10	Public Excursion Fare

7.6 Marketing Applications

1	A	Largest market: beach holidays (vacations)
2	C	Smallest market: diving holidays (vacations)
3	D	Most susceptible: holiday (vacation) visits
4	C	Least susceptible: business visits
5	A/D	Convenience products (CP)
6	B/C	Shopping products (SP)
7	D	Strongest image: Scotland among Canadian residents
8	C	Weakest image: Wales among Japanese residents
9	B	Largest market: a national women's magazine
10	C	Smallest market: a periodical for birdwatchers

7.7 Promotional Illustrations

1	Differential pricing
2	Transport advertising
3	Product segmentation
4	Publicity
5	Branding
6	Differential pricing
7	Direct mail
8	Classified advertising
9	Sales promotion
10	Merchandising

7.8 Creative Marketing Campaigns and Messages

1	Burger King
2	New York State

3	Holiday Inn International
4	American Express
5	Tourism Canada in the USA
6	British Airways
7	British Virgin Islands Tourist Board
8	British Tourist Authority in the USA
9	AVIS
10	United Airlines

7.9   Marketing Synonyms and Opposites

1	direct response marketing
2	personal selling
3	target marketing
4	merchandising
5	telemarketing
6	brand loyalty
7	sellers' market
8	desk research
9	planned economy
10	strategic marketing

7.10 Marketing Abbreviations and Acronyms

1	Attention, Interest, Desire, Action
2	computer reservation system/central reservation system
3	customer satisfaction questionnaire
4	direct response marketing
5	global distribution system
6	point of sale
7	public relations
8	resale price maintenance
9	Strengths, Weaknesses, Opportunities, Threats
10	unique selling proposition

Part 8
Planning and Development in Tourism

8.1 Basic Concepts

1 A National development plan with tourism as one of the sectors
2 B Inbound tourism followed by domestic tourism
3 B To establish the exact purpose for which it is required
4 B an approach to tourism in which local residents participate in its planning and development
5 A capacity of a site or area
6 C Swimming and scuba diving
7 B Cluster development strategy
8 C tourism activities which are in harmony with the environment in the long term
9 A Infrastructure
   B Infrastructure
   C Superstructure
10 B Alternative tourism

8.2 Resources

1 B better suited for tourism than for other economic activities
2 C They are (not) vulnerable
3 C Protecting something from decay and destruction
4 B Manpower
5 C Tourism
6 B Developed infrastructure
7 B As second homes (A and C denote permanent residence)
8 B Latitude
9 C Tourist information services
10 A Agriculture and tourism

8.3 Techniques, Systems and Processes

1	feasibility study
2	investment appraisal
3	Cost Benefit Analysis (CBA)
4	Programme Evaluation and Review Technique (PERT)
5	Critical Path Analysis (CPA)/network analysis
6	environmental audit
7	environmental impact assessment
8	energy management
9	water management
10	waste management

8.4 Ownership and Management

1	B	Involvement of two or more parties in ownership, management and operation of a business with a participation in the financial outcome
2	B	Right to use land or premises on certain conditions
3	B	Lease
4	C	Provision of organizational and operational expertise to manage a business by an operator for an agreed remuneration
5	A	Franchise
6	B	Owners and lenders (inter alia, in the use the business makes of its assets and in the relationship between owners' capital and loans)
7	A	an establishment
8	A	employee buy-out
9	B	investment in land and buildings and in interior assets
10	B	Condominium

8.5 Reshaping Existing Locations

1	Brighton
2	Bermuda
3	Bournemouth
4	Atlantic City
5	Scheveningen
6	Glasgow
7	Bradford
8	Montreal

9   Barcelona
10   Baltimore

8.6 Planning and Development Applications

1 B Faneuil Hall, Boston, Massachusetts
2 B Lake District National Park, Cumbria, England
3 D Venice, Italy
4 D Pomun Lake Resort, Republic of Korea
5 C growth of holidays (vacations) in the Mediterranean
6 B It has concentrated tourists into specific locations
7 C often arrested or slowed down by tourism development
8 C Tourism destroys industrial heritage
9 B Ramsar Sites
10 B 1960s

8.7 Planning and Development Terms

1   Sale and lease-back
2   Turnkey contract
3   Zoning
4   Tender
5   Public utilities
6   Ribbon development
7   Investment incentives
8   Land use planning/physical planning
9   Conservation areas/protected areas
10 Social cost

8.8 Planning and Development Synonyms and Opposites

1   appropriate technology/intermediate technology
2   rural planning
3   network analysis
4   interval ownership/multi-ownership
5   town planning

6   exclave
7   superstructure
8   social cost
9   public sector
10   rural planning

8.9 Planning and Development in the UK

1   United Kingdom (= Great Britain + Northern Ireland)
2   Town and Country Planning Act 1947
3   bylaws/by-laws/byelaws
4   unitary authorities
5   unitary development plans
6   Green Belts
7   Enterprise Zones
8   Urban Development Corporations
9   Tourism Development Action Plans (TDAPs)
10   Aviemore, Scotland (in 1966)

8.10 Conservation Areas and Schemes in the UK

		England	Scotland	Wales	N. Ireland
1	Areas of Outstanding Natural Beauty	✓		✓	✓
2	Conservation Areas	✓	✓	✓	
3	Heritage Coasts	✓		✓	
4	Listed Buildings	✓	✓	✓	
5	National Scenic Areas		✓		
6	National Nature Reserves	✓	✓	✓	✓
7	National Parks	✓		✓	
8	Scheduled Ancient Monuments	✓	✓	✓	✓
9	Sites of Special Scientific Interest	✓	✓	✓	✓
10	Special Protected Areas	✓			

Part 9
Organization and Finance in Tourism

9.1 Types of Organizations

1	motoring organization (also automobile association/club)
2	chamber of commerce
3	classification society
4	consortium/cooperative
5	federation
6	personnel association
7	professional body
8	tourist board
9	trade association
10	trade union (labor union in USA)

9.2 Governments and Tourism Organizations

1	C	Economic growth
	D	Employment
2	B	Employment
	C	Quality of environment
3	B	They are concerned with particular industries (i.e. sectors)
4	A	Local (based on resorts)
5	C	New Zealand (1901, France 1910, Switzerland 1917, Italy 1919)
6	C	Marketing/promotion
7	B	Need to promote destinations
8	B	In the Second World
9	D	Maximizing visitor revenue and resident employment
10	D	influence the policies of governments in relation to tourism

9.3 Organization of Tourism in the UK

1	B	1929 (grant of £5,000 by the Board of Trade)
2	A	England (English Tourist Board was established in 1969)
3	C	National Heritage (since 1992)
4	D	They are co-equal bodies
5	D	Northern Ireland Tourist Board (NITB, established under Development of Tourist Traffic Act (Northern Ireland) 1948)
6	C	Part III providing powers for statutory registration of tourist accommodation (Section 17)
7	B	Scottish Tourist Board (STB £18.4m, WTB £14.7m, NITB £14.7m, ETB £10.0m in 1996/97)
8	B	Scotland
9	C	Wales (in 1990)
10	D	Other commercial income (£17.7m, ETB £5.6m, LAs £2.0m, commercial membership £2.0m in 1995/96)

9.4 Tourism Organization in the UK and Irish Republic

1	Scotland
2	Wales
3	Northern Ireland
4	England
5	England
6	Department of Transport and Tourism (since 1987)
7	Bord Failte/Irish Tourist Board
8	Six (eight until 1984 when the Dublin and Eastern region were merged; in 1988 the functions of the Midwest RTO were incorporated in Shannon Development)
9	Council for Education, Recruitment and Training (CERT)
10	Irish Tourist Industry Confederation

9.5 International Organizations

1	ETC = NGO
2	IATA = NGO
3	ICAO = IGO

4   PATA = NGO
5   WTO = IGO
6   Membership of individuals and corporate bodies = NGO
7   Created by treaties = IGO
8   Subject to law of country of headquarters = NGO
9   Subject to international law = IGO
10   Able to take binding decisions = NGO

9.6   Finance in Tourism

1   A   Market economy
         B   Planned economy
         C   Mixed economy
2   B   Public sector
3   B   Increased value of sites leased or sold to investors
4   C   Visitor attractions
5   A   Reduction of capital outlay
6   B   Reduction of operating costs
7   C   Private developers and investors
8   B   Marketing/promotion
9   A   Central government
10   C   Raising revenue

9.7   International Sources of Finance

1   African/Asian Development Bank
2   Arab Fund for Economic and Social Development
3   Central American Bank for Economic Integration
4   Caribbean Development Bank
5   European Bank for Reconstruction and Development
6   European Development Fund
7   European Investment Bank
8   International Bank for Reconstruction and Development
9   Inter-American Development Bank
10   International Finance Corporation

9.8 Abbreviations of UK Organizations

1 Association of British Travel Agents
2 British Hospitality Association
3 Civil Aviation Authority
4 Hotel and Catering International Management Association
5 Institute of Leisure and Amenity Management
6 Northern Ireland Tourist Board
7 Passenger Shipping Association
8 National Union of Rail, Maritime and Transport Workers
9 Welsh Development Agency
10 Youth Hostels Association (England and Wales)

9.9 Abbreviations of US Organizations

1 American Automobile Association
2 American Bus Association
3 American Hotel & Motel Association
4 American Society of Travel Agents
5 Federal Aviation Administration
6 National Restaurant Association
7 National Tour Association
8 Travel Industry Association of America
9 Travel and Tourism Research Association
10 United States Tour Operators Association

9.10 UK versus US Financial Terms

1 bill
2 inventory
3 inventory turnover
4 accounts receivable
5 accounts payable
6 stock
7 common stock
8 preferred stock
9 payroll
10 leverage

Part 10
Miscellaneous Topics

10.1 Countries and Currencies

1	Schilling (s)
2	Danish Krone (Kr)
3	Deutsche Mark (DM)
4	Hong Kong Dollar (HK$)
5	Indian Rupee (Rs)
6	Italian Lira (L)
7	Netherlands Guilder (Fl)
8	Zloty
9	Portuguese Escudo (Esc)
10	Spanish Peseta (Pta)

10.2 Currencies and Countries

1	Greece
2	Netherlands (Guilder)
3	Czech Republic/Slovakia
4	Finland
5	Nigeria
6	South Africa
7	Belarus/Russian Federation/Tajikistan
8	Slovenia
9	North and South Korea
10	Japan

10.3 Employment Terms

1	Self-employment
2	Moonlighting

3	Black/hidden/informal economy
4	Ghosting
5	Teleworking
6	Casual/occasional employment
7	Flexitime
8	Job sharing
9	Split shift
10	Spreadover of hours

10.4 Nautical Terms

1	(ab)aft/(a)stern
2	bow/forward/prow
3	(a)midship(s)
4	port
5	starboard
6	leeward
7	windward
8	draft/draught
9	beam
10	abeam

10.5 Food and Catering Terms

1	kosher
2	halal
3	convenience food
4	table d'hôte menu
5	à la carte menu
6	brunch
7	American service/plate service
8	gueridon
9	French service
10	food court (also hawker centre in South-East Asia)

10.6 Airlines and Hotels, 1945–1995

Airline	1	2	3	4	5	6	7	8	9	10
Hotel co.	B	G	E	A	H	F	C	D	J	I

Aer Lingus   Copthorne Hotels
Air France   Meridien Hotels
Air India   Hotel Corporation of India
All Nippon Airways   Ana Enterprises
Japan Airlines   Nikko Hotels International
Pan American   Inter-Continental Hotels
SAS   Sunwing Hotels
TWA   Hilton International
United Airlines   Westin Hotels
VARIG   Tropical Hotels

10.7 Tourism and Technology

1   Facsimile transmission/fax
2   Videotex
3   Electronic funds transfer
4   Electronic ticketing
5   Virtual reality
6   Amadeus
7   Fantasia
8   Sabre
9   Worldspan
10 Apollo

10.8 US versus UK Language

1   full board/en pension
2   direct selling
3   queue jumping
4   in-house travel agency
5   timesharing
6   single ticket

7   berth
8   underground railway
9   transport café
10   post code

10.9 UK Leaders in the Tourism Industry

1   British Airways
2   London Heathrow (54.1 million terminal passengers in 1995)
3   Southend-on-Sea, Essex (2.15 km long; longest pier in the world)
4   Britannia Airways (owned by Thomson Corporation together with Thomson Holidays and Lunn Poly)
5   P&O (announced merger with Stena, second largest, in 1996; merger referred to Monopolies & Mergers Commission)
6   London Forum Hotel (in Cromwell Road, with accommodation for up to 1,856 guests in 910 rooms)
7   Forte (market share 20%+ of hotel rooms in 1995, acquired by Granada in 1996)
8   Thomson Holidays (estimated market share 30% in 1995)
9   Lunn Poly (800 retail outlets in 1996, Going Places 700+, A.T. Mays 400+, Thos. Cook 400)
10   Blackpool Pleasure Beach (with 7.4 million visitors in 1995)

10.10 World Leaders in the Tourism Industry

1   Delta Airlines (carried 87 million passengers in 1995 on 4,800 daily flights to 48 US States and 31 countries)
2   Chicago O'Hare (handled 67.3 million passengers in 1995)
3   *Norway* (Norwegian Cruise Line flagship 315m long with a capacity of 2,022 passengers and 900 crew)
4   MGM Grand Hotel/Casino in Las Vegas, Nevada, USA (with 5,005 rooms)
5   London Heathrow (46.8 million international passengers in 1995)
6   McDonald's International (owned and licensed 18,380 restaurants in 89 countries at the end of 1995)
7   West Edmonton Mall, Alberta, Canada (recorded 20 million shoppers in 1995)
8   Indian Railways (with 1.6 million employees in 1995)
9   *Silja Europa* between Stockholm, Sweden and Helsinki, Finland (can carry 3,000 passengers, 350 cars and 60 lorries)
10   Walt Disney World/Epcot Center, Florida, USA

Select Bibliography

All Parts

Medlik, S. (1996) *Dictionary of Travel, Tourism and Hospitality*, 2nd edn, Oxford: Butterworth–Heinemann

Part 1   Anatomy of Tourism

Burkart, A.J. and Medlik, S. (1981) *Tourism – Past, Present and Future*, 2nd edn, London: Heinemann, chs 4 and 5

McIntosh, R., Goeldner, C. and Ritchie, B. (1995) *Tourism: Principles, Practices, Philosophies*, 7th edn, New York: John Wiley

World Tourism Organization (1993) *Recommendations on Tourism Statistics*, Madrid: WTO

United Nations/World Tourism Organization (1995) *Recommendations on Tourism Statistics*, New York: United Nations

Part 2   Historical Development of Tourism

Burkart, A.J. and Medlik, S. (1990) *Historical Development of Tourism*, Les Cahiers du Tourisme Série C No. 143, Aix-en-Provence: Centre des Hautes Études Touristiques

Holloway, J.C. (1994) *The Business of Tourism*, 4th edn, London: Pitman, chs 2 and 3

Towner, J. (1996) *An Historical Geography of Recreation and Tourism in the Western World 1540–1940*, Chichester: John Wiley

Part 3   Geography of Tourism

Boniface, B.G. and Cooper, C.P. (1994) *The Geography of Travel and Tourism*, 2nd edn, Oxford: Butterworth–Heinemann

Hudman, L.E. and Jackson, R.H. (1994) *Geography of Travel and Tourism*, 2nd edn, Albany, NY: Delmar Publishers

Pearce, D. (1995) *Tourism Today: A Geographical Analysis*, 2nd edn, Harlow: Longman

Part 4   Dimensions of Tourism

British Tourist Authority (intermittent) *Digest of Tourism Statistics*, London: BTA

Cooper, C., Fletcher, J., Gilbert, D. and Wanhill, S. (1993) *Tourism: Principles and Practice*, London: Pitman, chs 6 and 7

Tourism Works for America Council (annual) *Tourism Works for America Annual Report*, Washington, DC

United Nations/World Tourism Organization (1995) *Recommendations on Tourism Statistics*, New York: United Nations

World Tourism Organization (annual) *Compendium of Tourism Statistics*, Madrid: WTO

See also text for particular statistical sources.

Part 5   Significance of Tourism

Bull, A. (1995) *The Economics of Travel and Tourism*, 2nd edn, Harlow: Longman

Cooper, C., Fletcher, J., Gilbert, D. and Wanhill, S. (1993) *Tourism: Principles and Practice*, London: Pitman, chs 10 and 11

Mathieson, A. and Wall, G. (1982) *Tourism: Economic, Physical and Social Impacts*, Harlow: Longman

Fridgen, J.D. (1991) *Dimensions of Tourism*, East Lansing, MI: Educational Institute of the American Hotel & Motel Association, chs 4, 6, 7

Tourism Works for America Council (annual) *Tourism Works for America Annual Report*, Washington, DC

Part 6   The Tourism Indistry

Cooper, C., Fletcher, J., Gilbert, D. and Wanhill, S. (1993) *Tourism: Principles and Practice*, London: Pitman, chs 15–18

Holloway, J.C. (1994) *The Business of Tourism*, 4th edn, London: Pitman, chs 7–13

Medlik, S. (1994) *The Business of Hotels*, 3rd edn, Oxford: Butterworth–Heinemann

Swarbrooke, J. (1995) *The Development and Management of Visitor Attractions*, Oxford: Butterworth–Heinemann

Tourism Works for America Council (annual) *Tourism Works for America Annual Report*, Washington, DC

Part 7   Marketing in Tourism

Middleton, V.T.C. (1994) *Marketing in Travel and Tourism*, 2nd edn, Oxford: Butterworth–Heinemann

Morrison, A.M. (1989) *Hospitality and Travel Marketing*, Albany, NY: Delmar Publishers

Witt, S.F. and Moutinho, L. (eds) (1994) *Tourism Marketing and Management Handbook*, 2nd edn, Part III, Hemel Hempstead: Prentice Hall

Part 8 Planning and Development in Tourism

Gunn, C.A. (1994) *Tourism Planning: Basics, Concepts, Cases*, 3rd edn, Washington, DC: Taylor and Francis

Innskeep, E. (1994) *National and Regional Tourism Planning – Methodologies and Case Studies*, London: Routledge

Pearce, D. (1989) *Tourist Development*, 2nd edn, Harlow: Longman

Part 9 Organization and Finance in Tourism

Burkart, A.J. and Medlik, S. (1981) *Tourism – Past, Present and Future*, 2nd edn, London: Heinemann, Part IX

Hollier, R. (1995) *The National and Regional Structures of Official Tourist Organisations in European Communities*, Paris: European Travel Commission

Pearce, D. (1992) *Tourist Organizations*, Harlow: Longman

Part 10 Miscellaneous Topics

Khan, M., Olsen, M. and Var, T. (eds) (1993) *VNR's Encyclopaedia of Hospitality and Tourism*, New York: Van Nostrand Reinhold

Medlik, S. (ed.) (1995) *Managing Tourism*, Oxford: Butterworth–Heinemann

Seaton, A.V. (ed.) (1994) *The State of the Art*, Chichester: John Wiley

Theobald, W. (ed.) (1995) *Global Tourism: The Next Decade*, Oxford: Butterworth–Heinemann

Witt, S.F. and Moutinho, L. (eds) (1994) *Tourism Marketing and Management Handbook*, 2nd edn, Hemel Hempstead: Prentice Hall

Index

Figures refer to questions using decimal numbering: the first figure denotes the Part of the book, the second the test within that Part, the third the question within that test. Thus, for example, 8.1.4 denotes Part 8 (Planning and Development in Tourism), test 1 (Basic Concepts), question 4 (community tourism). Names of individuals, organizations, countries and groups of countries are listed; lesser geographical entities are normally referred to only by names of the countries, in which they are to be found.